Studying for Science

Studying for Science

A guide to information, communication and study techniques

Brian White

Senior Lecturer
Humberside Polytechnic

E. & F.N. SPON
An imprint of Chapman and Hall
LONDON • NEW YORK • TOKYO • MELBOURNE • MADRAS

UK	Chapman and Hall, 2–6 Boundary Row, London SE1 8HN
USA	Chapman and Hall, 29 West 35th Street, New York NY 10001
JAPAN	Chapman and Hall Japan, Thomson Publishing Japan, Hirakawacho Nemoto Building, 7F, 1-7-11 Hirakawa-cho, Chiyoda-ku, Tokyo 102
AUSTRALIA	Chapman and Hall Australia, Thomas Nelson Australia, 480 La Trobe Street, PO Box 4725, Melbourne 3000
INDIA	Chapman and Hall India, R. Seshadri, 32 Second Main Road, CIT East, Madras 600 035

First edition 1991

© 1991 B. White

Typeset in 10/12pt Palatino by EJS Chemical Composition, Bath, Avon
Printed in Great Britain by Page Brothers Limited, Norwich, Norfolk

ISBN 0 419 14810 8   (HB)
ISBN 0 419 14820 5   (PB)

British Library Cataloguing in Publication Data

White, B.
    Effective skills for the science student.
    1.
    I. Title
    000.0

    ISBN 0–419–14810–8
        0–419–14820–5 Pbk

Library of Congress Cataloging-in-Publication Data

White, B.
    Effective skills for the science student.
      p. cm.
    Includes bibliographical references.
    ISBN 0–419–14810–8
        0–419–14820–5 Pbk
    1.   . 2.   .
    3.   . I. Title
00000.000 1990
000.0'000—dc00

00–0000
CIP

To Matthew

Contents

Preface

Looking back to when I started teaching, some 20 years ago, I am sure I was too critical of students' work. They were penalized not only for their lack of scientific knowledge and understanding, but also for failure in the way they approached their work and their inability to retrieve and use information. With hindsight, I realize that many of their supposed faults were of my own making. As a science teacher it was my job not only to extend and broaden subject knowledge, but also to instruct in the ways of studying science and demonstrate the accessibility of scientific information. I took for granted that they had already developed the skills of being a student; failing to appreciate that for many, unless told otherwise, academic work equated with a parrot-like ability to recall fact and detail.

With this in mind and after working for a number of years in the information, communication and study skills area, I decided to write a book specifically for science students. Although many skills books are published, the majority are for the humanities student, few are produced for the scientist.

In this book I have kept the content very wide. For example, in Chapter 3, Sources of scientific information, a number of information sources have been explained (some might say too many) in the hope that students will appreciate that information is readily available in different forms. Many students, even at degree level, become too reliant on textbooks as their only information source. With Chapter 9, How to plan and carry out projects, surveys have been counted as a type of practical investigation. Some scientists consider surveys as unacceptable scientific work. I disagree, and would argue that a properly conducted survey can generate primary information which is just as valid as that from a more traditional scientific experiment. With the increased interest and concern about the interaction of science and society, surveys are a valuable method for scientists to use. Although computers are mentioned with reference to on-line searching, CD-ROMs and word processing, a separate section on them is not included. This is because students are becoming increasingly familiar with computers and a number of good books are readily available.

Throughout the book I have used words like 'student', 'teacher' and 'college' in their widest sense: 'college' is taken to include any university, school or institute of further and higher education. A student is anyone, at any age, on a science course, and a teacher may be a university lecturer, school master/mistress, demonstrator – in fact anyone involved in the teaching of students.

I must thank a large number of people who have helped in the production of this book. The staff of E. & F.N. Spon, especially Madeleine Metcalfe, for sound professional advice. My colleagues and friends Barrie Donn, Ian Franklin, Robin and Christine Storey and Chris Robinson for reading the entire manuscript and producing many helpful comments. Thanks are also due to Joy Watson for advice with Chapters 7 and 9, to Mandy Smith for help with Chapters 3 and 4, and Gary Wheatley for assistance with the Appendix. A special thank you goes to my wife, Margaret, my son, Matthew, and my step-mother, Iris. They have been a constant source of encouragement and practical help at all stages in the preparation of the book.

This book contains lots of advice and unfortunately advice sometimes seems patronizing in the sense of condescension. Patronizing also means to offer support and encouragement, and the book was written very much in this spirit. If it reads in any way superior or aloof this was not the intention. Finally, after using the book if you have any comments or criticisms then I shall be only too pleased to hear from you.

Brian White
Humberside Polytechnic
Cottingham Road
Hull
HU6 7RT

1

What this book is about

1.1 INTRODUCTION

This book has been written to help science students with their studies. As a student you may be on a GCSE course, studying GCE advanced level, enrolled on a BTEC programme, an undergraduate, a mature student returning to study via an Access or Flexistudy programme, or following an open or distance learning course. In fact this book is for anyone studying science who feels in need of some guidance in achieving the best from their course.

You may wonder how this type of book can help, and this needs some explanation. In recent years science courses have changed in approach, in that there is less emphasis on memorizing large amounts of information. Many other things are assessed and examination syllabuses sometimes refer to these as 'assessment objectives'. In syllabuses, objectives are written in a very formal style and may appear as follows:

Candidates should be able to:

* Understand and explain theories about scientific phenomena, and say why they are important.
* Search out, select, organize and communicate scientific information in the form of assignments such as essays, talks and projects.
* Design and carry out scientific investigations, observing, measuring, and recording the results, and comparing them with those collected by other scientists.
* Display and arrange data in a suitable form such as graphs and figures.
* Analyse and interpret scientific data, and discuss any apparent trends and conclusions.
* Use formulae and make calculations.
* Achieve a level of competence in the practical skills associated with science.
* Realize the importance of science to society and have an awareness of the applications of science.

Such a list is quite formidable and intimidating. Don't be put off. It simply means, in order to be successful on a course, you need to demonstrate a range of different skills. For example, when working on an assignment, for example an essay, you must search out relevant information, work through it, usually by making notes, prepare tables and figures, and finally write and present the assignment in a suitable form.

Course work is also becoming more important in determining progress and on some courses accounts for between 20–30% of the final grade awarded. Pass or fail, therefore, does not depend solely on time spent in the examination room. This is fairer, since it means that all aspects of work are taken into account. It also means, however, that you need to become an independent learner, willing and able to be self-directed and having the confidence to take charge of your own studying. This book helps you achieve this by giving advice on how to tackle the different tasks you need to do.

1.2 HOW TO USE THE BOOK

The book is a guide and, depending on your experience, you may not require every chapter. To help you select the parts you need a key is provided (see p. 3). To assist further, various sections of the book are cross-referenced and the page numbers given. Any examples have been kept very simple to emphasize the points they make. Also every chapter has a summary highlighting important features. Remember that many study, communication and information skills are very much interrelated. For instance, it would be difficult to complete a project (Chapter 9, p. 155) without having first developed and practised information skills (Chapters 4 and 5, p. 59 and 72), as well as having some knowledge of presentation (Chapter 6, p. 87). It is also easier to complete many assignments if the work can be divided into a number of stages, and advice on how to do this is included.

1.3 ACHIEVING SUCCESS

The key to academic success is organization and the willingness to work hard. Instant learning does not exist! To an uninformed outsider seeing students in a library sitting at tables surrounded with books and paper, studying must seem deceptively easy. This is anything but the case: it takes commitment, motivation and the will to succeed, demanding a great deal of time and effort. All through your course, take a positive attitude. Be enthusiastic and determined to achieve the best results you are capable. Studying is an active process – the more you put into it, the more you get out of it. Regard it as an opportunity not to be missed. Successful studying always gives a sense of achievement and satisfaction.

It makes time at college more enjoyable if you make friends with other members of the class and also the staff who teach you. Take no notice of pressure groups who think studying and working hard is a waste of time. Be an independent learner and do what is right for you. As far as the staff are concerned remember they are there to help you, so work with them and not against them. Never be afraid to ask for a teacher's help and take full advantage of any extra revision classes which may be organized. Although most teachers are more than willing to solve a student's problems, if you have a lot of questions it is a good idea to make an appointment, rather than catch them at the end of a class. They may be rushed and short of time to get to their next lesson. Also remember that teachers are not mind readers; you need to tell them of any difficulties. Always go and see them and get things sorted out. Science is often progressive, in that fact A needs to be explained before fact B may be understood, and so on. It is impossible to appreciate and learn something which you don't understand. Never try to.

Lastly, many students spend a great deal of time working through study skills and similar type books, but never put the advice into practice. Do try the various techniques described here and use the information given. They will prove a great help. Studying is on-going; the more you do the easier it becomes. Although this book will go a long way in helping you with your work, it may not solve every query. With this in mind a bibliography (see p. 185) is included.

1.4 KEY

By answering the appropriate question(s) the following key will direct you to the part(s) of the book dealing with your query. The key has been constructed so that you may arrive at the same page by more than one route.

Question 1 – GETTING STARTED

I need help with:

* basic skills and needs . . . . **Go to question 2**
* written work and other assignments . . . . **Go to question 4**
* examinations . . . . **Go to question 7**
* finding information . . . . **Go to question 8**
* preparing a talk . . . . **Go to question 11**
* a long piece of independent work . . . . **Go to question 12**
* displaying results and other data (i.e. tables, graphs, pie charts etc.)
. . . . **Go to question 15**

Question 2 – THE BASICS

I need help with:

* choosing the equipment and facilities needed for studying . **Go to page 8**
* organizing my time in order to study effectively . . . . . **Go to page 9**
* improving my reading techniques . . . . **Go to page 14**
* making notes . . . . **Go to page 12**
* practical work . . . . **Go to page 16**
* working with other students . . . . **Go to page 17**

Question 3 – NOTE-TAKING

I need help when:

* making notes in a class/lecture . . . . **Go to page 12**
* making notes from books and other information sources . **Go to page 13**
* choosing a style of note-making . . . . **Go to page 14**

Question 4 – WRITTEN WORK

I need help when:

* using quotations, compiling a bibliography, presenting, etc.
  . . . . **Go to question 5**
* planning and writing-up assignments. . . . . **Go to question 6**

Question 5 – POINTS OF STYLE

I need help with:

* quoting references. **Go to page 112**
* compiling a bibliography. . . . . **Go to page 113**
* the use of quotations, footnotes, etc. . . . . **Go to page 116**
* setting out tables and figures and displaying data . **Go to question 15**

Question 6 – ASSIGNMENT

I need help with:

* an essay
  To sort out the information needed . . . . **Go to page 73**
  to prepare and write it up . . . . **Go to page 100**

* a class practical
    to sort out the information needed . . . . Go to page 75
    to prepare and write it up . . . . Go to page 102
* a long term practical assignment (e.g. project)
    to sort out the information needed . . . . Go to page 75
    to prepare and write it up . . . . Go to page 102
* a long term non-practical assignment (e.g. dissertation)
    to sort out the information needed . . . . Go to page 74
    to prepare and write it up . . . . Go to page 109

Question 7 – EXAMS

I need help with:

* planning my revision . . . . Go to page 171
* with examination techniques (e.g. choice of questions, planning answers, etc.) . . . . Go to page 174

Question 8 – INFORMATION SOURCES

I need help to:

* find what different information sources are available   Go to question 9
* search out the different information sources . . . .   Go to question 10

Question 9 – LOCATING INFORMATION

I need help to:

* find sources containing new and original information . . . Go to page 20
* find sources containing second-hand information . . . . Go to page 32
* locate what book sources are available . . . . Go to page 33
* locate what non-book sources (e.g. film) are available . . . Go to page 42

Question 10 – INFORMATION AND LIBRARIES

I need help to:

* understand how libraries classify and catalogue their stock
    . . . . Go to page 59
* identify and sort out my information needs . . . . Go to page 77

* choose the type of information required for the following
   an essay . . . . **Go to page 73**
   practical work . . . . **Go to page 75**
   a dissertation . . . . **Go to page 74**
   everyday class work . . . . **Go to page 76**

Question 11 – GIVING A TALK

I need help:

* to plan and prepare a talk . . . . **Go to page 145**
* in choosing which information sources to use . . . . . . **Go to page 76**
* to write the notes to use during a talk . . . . **Go to page 148**
* with the visual aids . . . . **Go to page 149**
* with the actual delivery . . . . **Go to page 152**

Question 12 – PROJECTS AND DISSERTATIONS

I need help to:

* complete a project (i.e. a long term practical assignment)
   . . . . **Go to question 13**
* complete a dissertation (i.e. a long term non-practical assignment)
   . . . . **Go to question 14**

Question 13 – PROJECTS

I need help:

* and general advice about a project . . . . **Go to page 155**
* deciding the information needs of a project . . . . **Go to page 75**
* to choose which type of project to do . . . . **Go to page 156**
* designing the practical work involved . . . . **Go to page 158**
* to display the results of a project . . . . **Go to question 15**
* writing up a project . . . . **Go to page 102**

Question 14 – DISSERTATIONS

I need help:

* and general advice about a dissertation . . . . **Go to page 74**
* deciding the information needs of a dissertation . . . . . **Go to page 74**
* writing up a dissertation . . . . **Go to page 109**

Question 15 – DISPLAYING DATA

I need help to:

* display numerical results . . . .   **Go to question 16**
* display non-numerical results . . . .   **Go to page 140**

Question 16 – TABLES, FIGURES AND STATISTICS

I need help:

* constructing tables   . . . .   **Go to page 121**
* to draw figures (graphs, bar charts, etc.) . . . .   **Go to page 125**
* when using statistics   . . . .   **Go to page 167**

2

Basic study skills

It is often taken for granted that most people can ride a bicycle. Studying is similar in that it is assumed all students have the ability and expertise to study. We forget that, like cycling, studying is a skill and at some point has to be learnt. Like any skill it improves with practice and confidence.

This chapter explains the basic skills and requirements you need. The topics dealt with are:

- requirements for study
- organizing your time
- making notes
- reading techniques
- practical work
- working in groups.

2.1 REQUIREMENTS FOR STUDY

In order to study you need:

○ A place to work. Most likely you will study either at home, or in a library. At home, find a room (possibly your bedroom) where you will be left undisturbed. No special equipment is needed apart from a table, chair, good lighting, heating and a supply of stationery. When working in a library find a quiet place away from the main issuing and cataloguing areas, since these tend to be noisy. Some libraries provide carrels (separate booths) which are particularly good. Try different parts of the library and decide which suits you the best. In a library you will always be aware of other readers; make a determined effort not to keep lifting your head to see who is about. If you do, this will hinder your train of thought and concentration.
○ Peace and quiet in order to keep your mind on the work. Although some students would disagree, effective studying is unlikely to take place with

either the TV set or hi-fi system turned on and the volume set at maximum.

○ A supply of plain, lined and graph paper. It is often cheaper to buy in the ream and it can be bought pre-punched to fit into ring files. Also, lined paper can be obtained with different line widths. Items of stationery can be bought at booksellers and office suppliers, and many larger colleges now have their own student shops.

○ Files for notes and practical work. Like paper, files come in different sizes – A4 (210 mm × 297 mm) is a good popular size. Some colleges prefer practical work to be written up in notebooks and advise on the best type. Several coloured files are also useful to separate notes when preparing assignments (see p. 85).

○ A set of pens, pencils and coloured crayons, or felt-tipped pens.

○ Paper clips, treasury tags and a stapler are useful for keeping papers together, especially when handing in work.

○ A diary or personal organizer and wall chart to plan your study schedule.

○ Record cards and a box in which to keep reference details.

○ A small notebook or pad to jot down ideas and short notes. If you have an organizer use this instead.

○ Calculator and mathematical instruments (e.g. pair of compasses, ruler, set square, protractor).

○ Laboratory coat and safety spectacles. Most colleges advise students on the style and where to buy. A laboratory coat needs regular washing, so one made of a fabric (e.g. polycotton) which launders easily is the best. Don't use a nylon coat – many organic solvents will soon dissolve it away.

○ A good dictionary and thesaurus. You may be recommended to buy some textbooks, in which case bear in mind the advice given on p. 40.

○ A good pair of scissors and some fast-drying paper adhesive is also useful.

○ Depending on your course you may need tables of scientific constants, units, symbols etc.

○ Biology students may need dissecting instruments. These are very expensive so ask your teacher what is needed before you buy.

2.2 ORGANIZING YOUR TIME

Studying science takes up a lot of time. In addition to lectures and practical sessions, there are assignments to prepare, examinations to revise for, as well as many other things which need doing. Time spent in class is insufficient on its own, and you must be prepared to set aside some of your own time if the academic work is to be successful. This is not always easy; part-time students may have full-time jobs, some full-time students take on weekend work, and those away from home often have domestic duties.

It is important, therefore, right at the start of a course, to organize your time sensibly and effectively.

How to plan your time

The following method is a good way of organizing your time. It is flexible and easily changed to suit individual needs.

1. Buy a diary – one arranged with a week displayed over 2 pages is best, since this gives more writing space. Remember that the education year runs from autumn to summer, and specially printed diaries are available. A good alternative is a personal organizer system.
2. Start by entering into the diary the opening and closing dates of each term.
3. Most courses provide a weekly timetable, so copy this in for the whole year. This may take some time, but it helps in the long run. If possible, distinguish between lectures, practicals, seminars etc. Some colleges operate a 6-day timetable; be careful when filling this into a diary.
4. Enter other important dates such as examinations and deadlines for handing in course work. If you have a set homework timetable, include this as well.
5. Rest and relaxation are important. If you belong to any clubs and societies, make a note of these, together with any special occasions, like birthdays, when you intend not to work.
6. If you have a job then include your hours of work.
7. By now the diary will be reasonably full. You will see at a glance how much time is spent in class and with hobbies etc. Next, go through each week and mark in any periods which can be used for private study. If possible find sessions of about 2–3 hours long. The amount of private study needed will depend on the level of the course; more advanced qualifications generally require more time; if you have a set homework timetable then this forms part of your private study time. A good guide is to spend as much time on private study as that spent in class. If this is not possible, then do the best you can. Remember, studying is hard work and your active commitment to it is essential if you want to succeed. Once you have identified your private study periods, keep them; only change them in extreme emergencies.

It is also helpful to find shorter periods of time; the odd quarter of an hour is fine for giving an essay a last read through or sorting out a number of references. If you travel by public transport, use the journey to sort out lecture notes and for examination revision. Don't waste free time at college with over-long coffee breaks; use these periods to search out books from the library or see teaching staff with queries.

All this helps with studying. You are using all the available time and approaching the course in an efficient, hard-working manner. This in turn increases your confidence and ability to study.

Using the private study periods

Having identified periods for private study, it is important to use them wisely. The first thing to remember is never work a 2–3 hour session without a break. By the end you will be overtired, confused and will have achieved very little. Instead, divide each study period into blocks of about 30 minutes. In each one concentrate and work as hard as you can. Ignore any outside noise and activity. At the end of 30 minutes have a short rest of about 5 minutes. In this break do two things.

1. In your mind, quickly run through the work just done; this helps recall.
2. Next, do something completely different. Have a quick drink, play your latest record, see what the family are doing.

After the short break return to work and repeat the same regime. A WORD OF CAUTION – never be tempted to extend this break longer than 5 minutes, otherwise little work will get done.

Having confidence in your ability to work independently is an important part of the studying process, and, in one complete study session, you will have spent approximately 2–3 hours on real concentrated effort. By adopting this pattern of work for all your studies, you will know you are working hard and well.

Other points about getting organized

○ A year planner or wall chart is a help. Mark on it term, vacation and all other dates. This helps plan the study programme over a year, whereas a diary keeps you informed of daily and weekly needs.
○ At the beginning of each week go through your diary and decide what has to be done during the coming week. Sort out what you need for each class (e.g. laboratory coat, safety spectacles, note books). Also decide what work you intend to do in the private study periods. Never over-estimate how much can be done – set yourself realistic goals and stick to them.
○ Vacation time should also be used. Although you need a good break after a hard term, use some of the holiday to revise the previous term's work and sort out its problems. Some courses even set special vacation assignments.
○ When studying in the evening try not to work too late. Regular sleep and rest are important.

o Occasionally you may get behind with the work and have to give up time normally set aside for another activity. Don't worry, since this happens to the best of students. However, if you always feel behind with the work, then take a careful look at your organization and see if it can be improved. If this offers little help, then have a serious talk with your teacher about the way you study. Some colleges have welfare and counselling staff who are experts at sorting out a student's problems. Go and see them and talk over any difficulties.

2.3 MAKING NOTES

The ability to make concise, clear notes is one of the most important skills you need when studying science. A good set of notes is invaluable; you will use them when writing up assignments and revising for examinations. The act of making notes, in itself, helps understanding and is a useful aid to memory.

Most likely you will make notes from lectures and books and other information sources. Some teachers dictate notes and even take them in to check and mark. If this applies to you, this section will still be useful when making notes from books etc.

Notes from lectures

o At the beginning of every lecture, write at the top of the paper the date, title of lecture and lecturer's name (you will then know who to contact should you need help later on).
o Never try to write down every word spoken in a lecture, even if the delivery is slow. Notes should be as short as possible, with only the main points written down. Listen, then write. For example, if the teacher says 'I'm going to discuss 4 aspects of this topic', you then know that the lecture is divided into four parts. Simply write the number 1 in the margin of your paper, then wait for what comes next. There is no point in writing any more at this stage. Always use your own words rather than copy down every word spoken. This helps understanding and recall.
o Abbreviate as much as possible, and gradually develop your own shorthand: for example
  * For 'therefore' write $\therefore$
  * For 'on account of/because' write $\because$
  * For 'into' write $\rightarrow$
  * For 'from' write $\leftarrow$
  * For 'physical properties' write   ph. props
  * For 'equation' write   eqn
  * For 'example' write   e.g.
  * For 'respiration' write   rsp.

* For 'precipitate' write   **ppt.**
* For 'combustion' write   **cmb.**
* For 'volume' write   **vol.**
Many students when making notes for the first time fear they will never remember what the abbreviations stand for. Don't worry, because you will if you are consistent. With science, many specialized terms turn up again and again, so you can gradually build up your own glossary of abbreviations.

o Notes are easier to recall if you underline headings and important words (coloured pens help here). Never do this in class as it takes up too much time. Underline when revising the notes after the lecture.

o As far as possible keep the notes in list form and number each point. Again the numbering can be done at the end of the lecture.

o Don't worry if the notes look untidy. Remember, notes are for your use only, and as long as you can understand them that is all that matters. Never copy out notes simply to make them look neat. This is very time-consuming, and achieves very little.

o As soon as possible after a lecture, revise and work through your notes. This is the time when you underline key words and headings, and number up the various sections. Be sure you understand what the lecture is all about. You cannot learn what you don't understand; check any difficult points with your teacher at the next available opportunity.

o Use plenty of paper, writing on one side only and every other line. Also, leave good margins. This may seem wasteful, but well-spaced notes are easier to read and learn. It also gives you lots of space to add extra information when you supplement the lecture material with additional background reading. Aim to have one set of notes for each topic. This ensures, when you revise, that all the information is in one place. It saves time in not having to chase up several files and books.

o Number every sheet of paper in case they become loose and fall out of a file.

o Unless needed, only take the previous lecture's notes to the next class. Files are bulky things to carry around and are easily mislaid. To lose a whole year's notes can be devastating, especially before an examination. Always keep them in a safe place.

o At the end of a series of lectures on one topic, condense the information from the notes and produce a one-page summary. Use the pattern style described below. These summaries are very helpful for examination revision (see p. 172).

Notes from books and other information sources

o Keep to the same style as used in lectures and incorporate new material into existing lecture notes, rather than make an extra set. Use the spare space left in your lecture notes.

○ Always read through any book or periodical etc. before you make any notes. Look out for the main points as you read, and make the notes on a second read through. Never copy out passages; rather, use your own words, since these will be easier to recall and understand. An exception is if you need a quotation, or are dealing with numerical data, in which case copy it out correctly. Always include quotations in quotation marks, so you can easily distinguish them: p. 116 gives advice about using quotations.

○ Keep a full record of any information source used (see p. 112).

○ After making notes, read through them to check that they are clear and that you can understand them. This is important if the book needs to be returned to the library by a certain date.

○ When using their own books some students prefer to mark up the book (normally in pencil) rather than make separate notes. Paragraphs can be numbered and the main points in the text underlined. Although this saves writing, it does mean that both book and lecture notes are needed when revising a topic. Also, if you want to sell the book at the end of a course, lots of marks may cause a reduction in the second-hand price.

Different styles of making notes

Most students write notes going down the page, i.e., linear notes. There are, however, other ways of arranging them and one popular method is to make pattern notes. These look similar to the brainstorming patterns described on p. 78. With pattern notes the title is written in the centre of the page and all the information goes around the edge, with lines and arrows linking each part. Figure 2.1 shows what the pattern note system would look like for the advice given in this chapter about making notes.

Both the linear and pattern systems are good; try them and see which you prefer. A good scheme is to use a combination of both styles. Linear notes are good for lectures and information from books, etc. The pattern system is excellent to make the one-page summaries useful for revision.

2.4 READING TECHNIQUES

Academic study involves a lot of reading, since most courses expect students to read around the subject, adding extra information and examples to the work covered in class. Different techniques have been developed which allow you to read quickly without losing any sense or meaning. Methods such as 'skim reading' and 'scan reading' can be helpful, and the bibliography lists books which describe these methods in detail. The following advice may also help.

Figure 2.1 'Pattern Note' summary on making notes.

○ Always sit comfortably and have a good light when doing a lot of reading. If you use spectacles, be sure you have the right correction.

○ Decide why you are reading in the first place. Is it for enjoyment (in which case take your time) or to collect information (in which case be as efficient as possible)?

○ Always use the contents and index sections of a book etc. to locate the parts you need. Rarely does a book need to be read from cover to cover.

○ If you are searching for certain information, make your eyes skim down the page looking for significant words and examples.
○ Try and reduce eye movement to a minimum. A ruler or finger going down the page as you read may help you concentrate and pick out the important points.
○ Try to read groups of words at a time rather than single words. Saying the words to yourself as you read also slows you down. An exception is when checking the final draft of any work; then read slowly in order to pick up any errors.
○ Authors' writing styles vary, and if you find a book or article particularly difficult, it may be more profitable to find an alternative source of information.

2.5 PRACTICAL WORK

Science is a practical subject and most students spend a good part of their course carrying out practical work. The term 'practical work' is a general one and does not always mean working in a laboratory. For example, an ecologist visits habitats such as the sea shore or moor collecting data. This is called fieldwork. The nature of the practical work can also vary. It may be either short exercises to demonstrate and back up theory work, or long-term independent investigations (usually called projects). Irrespective of the type of practical work, there are a number of points to remember and, in general, these refer to safety and good working practice.

Science, like any practical subject, can be hazardous and simple techniques not properly carried out prove dangerous. However, with care and attention to detail, science is no more dangerous than any other practical subject. In the UK, Acts of Parliament and Government regulations, e.g. Control of Substances Hazardous to Health Regulations, 1988 (COSHH), control the type of work which can be done. All colleges must have codes of practice and guidelines which must be followed. These include the correct handling and storage of chemicals, the use of protective clothing, the correct use of equipment, the disposal of waste substances, the use of compressed gases, electrical hazards, the prohibition of eating and smoking etc.

Before carrying out any practical work, know exactly what you have to do and ask if you are uncertain. Never be a danger to yourself and other students.

Well organized practical work is an essential and exciting part of any science course where you can discover, at first hand, what science is really all about. Because practical work is so important it is referred to in other parts of the book. For example, Chapter 6 (p. 113) gives advice on the presentation of practical work and Chapter 9 (p. 155) is about projects.

2.6 WORKING IN GROUPS

In science you will sometimes work closely with other students on your course. Often in practical classes you will need to be in small groups, especially if certain equipment has to be shared. You may be able to choose your partner(s), although in some classes you will be allocated to a particular group. Either way it is important when working with other students that you adopt, from the beginning, a friendly yet professional, business-like relationship. Each student must contribute an equal amount of effort to the job in hand. This means, for example, taking turns to wash glassware, make up solutions, observe and take readings etc.

Some courses include non-practical group work where students between them research a particular topic and present it as a report or talk. Certain examination boards regard this type of activity as essential, and refer to it as 'the development of inter-personal skills'.

Working with other students, if well organized, can be fun and profitable. You will help and support each other, exchange ideas and feel part of a team. However, when working in a group decide at the start exactly what needs to be done, giving each other specific tasks, so that you arrive at a shared workload. With long assignments, arrange to meet at regular intervals so that you can check on progress and, if necessary, reallocate the different jobs. Examination revision can also be carried out in a group and this is described on p. 174.

SUMMARY

This chapter covers the basic skills and requirements needed for successful study. Aim to become an independent and effective learner.

The key points are:

- check you have all the equipment you need
- organize your time now and identify long and short term study periods – try using the 30 minute and 5 minute method of working
- practise making notes: experiment with the different styles of note making and see which you prefer, and don't be afraid to abbreviate
- make a determined effort to read faster – it really does work
- be methodical and careful with practical work
- be professional when working with other students – adopt a co-operative and business-like manner
- enjoy your course – success means satisfaction.

3

Sources of scientific information

This chapter is about scientific information. Information is present in many forms – books, periodicals, computer databases and videos – and the amount is increasing all the time. Before you can use information effectively, there are a number of things to consider.

○ The different types of scientific information which are available, their uses, limitations and how to locate them.
○ How libraries store, classify and catalogue their scientific stock. The ability to search out information quickly saves time and speeds up a study schedule.
○ How to identify particular information needs. If you have an essay to write, a project to plan, or wish to revise a topic, how do you decide which are the best information sources to use?

This chapter is mainly concerned with the first of these and it is described under the following headings:

- the importance of scientific information
- types of scientific information
- primary book sources
- secondary book sources
- non-book sources.

3.1 THE IMPORTANCE OF SCIENTIFIC INFORMATION

Information is very important to a science student. You need it to:

* Supplement class work.
* Help in the preparation of assignments.
* Design practical investigations and check, for example, on the apparatus and reagents which may be needed.

* Verify specific queries like names of chemical compounds, physical constants and formulae.
* Make your own notes on a topic not being taught in class, often the case if you are on a distance-learning course.
* Work over and revise a topic you find difficult to understand.
* Provide background material when beginning a new subject.

In addition, the gathering and understanding of scientific information will increase your subject knowledge. You will be able to arrive at more informed decisions; accurate and correct information helps you judge a situation for yourself.

3.2 TYPES OF SCIENTIFIC INFORMATION

Information may be categorized into primary and secondary material. If information is new and has never been published before it is termed **primary**. It includes original research, new legislation and survey results, like government statistics. Primary information is always up-to-date, detailed, accurate and specialized. Consequently, fewer people want to use it and it tends to be expensive.

Information produced when scientists re-work primary material for a special purpose, like writing a skills textbook, or compiling an encyclopaedia, is termed **secondary** information. As a result secondary publications tend to be less specialized and cheaper to buy. They have a wider readership and are more accessible. It takes time to go through a great many primary sources and mistakes may be made in copying out data. Secondary work is, therefore, sometimes out-of-date and inaccurate. This is not to deny the value of textbooks and similar material – they are an excellent source of information. You should, however, be aware of their limitations.

It is important that you can recognize and distinguish new information from old. This is often difficult; a scientist when describing new research results (primary information) may refer to, and comment on, work published by others (secondary information).

The different information sources described in this chapter have been divided into book and non-book categories. Sources which are published in a printed form, such as periodicals, textbooks and government reports, are termed **book** sources. The book sources are further divided into primary and secondary types to help you separate new from second-hand information.

Other material, including maps, audio-visual items, online searching and organizations, is **non-book** material. Although termed non-book sources, information about them is usually found in books and catalogues etc.

The main points about each source are explained, with advice on how to find them. Their uses and limitations are also described. You may not need every source mentioned in this book – this will depend on your course and the assignments you are set. Scientific information is, however, growing at an alarming rate, and, in the future, you may be on a different course, or have a job where you will be expected to use the full range of material. It is, therefore, a good idea to learn about it now. Also, a working knowledge will help you be more selective when searching out information (Chapter 5, p. 72), and assist you in its writing up and presentation (Chapter 6, p. 87).

All the indexes, guides and catalogues etc. listed are generally well known, and should be found in many public and academic libraries. Although the publication dates were as up-to-date as possible at the time of writing, it is always best to use the latest editions available. Nearly all have instructions on how to use them – follow these carefully. Any bibliographical details given are arranged according to the formats explained in Chapter 6 (see p. 114). Reference is also made to the Inter Library Loan (ILL) service and this is described on page 67.

3.3 PRIMARY BOOK SOURCES

Primary book sources include conference proceedings, official publications, patents, periodicals, reports, research in progress, standards, statistics, theses and trade literature.

Conference proceedings

Scientific organizations, associations and learned societies often arrange conferences to which scientists are invited to give lectures about their research. These lectures are written up as articles (scientists refer to articles as **scientific papers**), and all papers from the same conference are collated and published in book form. Conferences are also called symposia, congresses, workshops, colloquia, or some other similar term.

Uses

* They are up-to-date in a particular research area and will help with projects and dissertations.
* Conference papers are a useful source of additional references.
* The information is detailed.

Limitations

* The information is specialized, and may not be needed for general class work.

* A library's stock will be limited, so the ILL service may be needed to obtain copies of particular papers.

How to locate

To trace what is available, the following is useful. This index lists conference proceedings from all over the world. It is well arranged and easy to use. It appears monthly, with annual cumulations. An 18-year cumulation (1964–81) is also available on microfiche (see p. 49). The index is also on-line through the BLAISE system (see p. 51). To date over 250 000 conferences have been listed in the index.

Index of Conference Proceedings Received. British Library Document Supply Centre, (BLDSC), Boston Spa (see p. 69)

Official publications

Governments and organizations like the European Economic Community (EEC) and World Health Organization (WHO) produce information for the scientist. A vast range is published on such topics as genetic engineering, computers, acid rain and other current issues.

In the UK the majority of official publications are produced by Her Majesty's Stationery Office (HMSO), although some government departments publish in their own right. Information about the day-to-day working of Parliament appears in parliamentary publications. This includes details of legislation, debate reports, and special reports known as Command Papers. There are also non-parliamentary publications which include departmental, technical and scientific reports.

Uses

* Useful for dissertations and work which requires a discussion of the wider issues of science, such as health, safety, economics and commercial applications.
* Official publications are accurate and precise.
* Well referenced and list other sources of information.
* Large libraries carry a good stock, so access is not normally a problem.

Limitations

* Written in a formal style which needs careful reading.
* The ILL service will be needed if you only have access to a small library.

How to locate

UK publications

Many HMSO catalogues are available. They also list publications of organizations, e.g. United Nations Educational, Scientific and Cultural Organisation (UNESCO), for which HMSO is the UK distributor. There are four common catalogues.

1. The *Daily List*, which lists all new HMSO documents for sale on that day. It normally appears every week from Monday to Friday. No subject index present.
2. A *monthly catalogue* is produced, and this has a subject index.
3. An *annual catalogue* is published, and this is a cumulation of the monthly lists. It contains subject, title and name indexes. This is the best guide to use when starting a search.
4. *Sectional lists* are also available. They are a series of catalogues containing details of publications from each government department. They are also indexed.

Many official documents, although not published by HMSO, are written by organizations, wholly or partly financed by the Government. These can be traced by using the *Catalogue of British Official Publications not Published by HMSO*, Chadwyck-Healey Ltd, Cambridge. This appears annually and is worth searching out. It is well indexed and easy to use.

EEC publications

The EEC produces information in large quantities and much is useful to the scientist. Certain libraries (over 50) in the UK are designated 'European Document Centres' and receive all EEC publications. Your local library should be able to tell you where your nearest centre is located. Most centres have special librarians to assist with enquiries.

Other countries

All countries produce official documents. You may not need any, but if you should, then the following is a good place to start your search:

Palic, V.M. (1977) *Government Publications: A Guide to Bibliographical Tools (incorporating Government Organisation Manuals: A bibliography). Guides to Official Publications, Volume I.* Pergamon Press, Oxford.

Other organizations

The current publications of organizations like the United Nations and WHO etc. can be traced using *British Books in Print* (BBIP). This is explained under Bibliographies on p. 32.

Patents

If you have a new idea which could be manufactured and sold, in order to protect the invention from pirating and unauthorized production, you need to obtain a **patent**. This is a legally enforceable monopoly granted to the inventor to stop others from making, selling, or using the invention without permission. In the UK patents are granted by the Patent Office, which is part of the Department of Trade and Industry. A patent is granted for a fixed number of years in return for a full description of the idea. These descriptions are stored and classified, and are available to the general public.

Patents are granted for a wide range of inventions from advanced electronics to a new type of screwdriver. In the UK a patent may only be granted for an idea which is new at the date the application is made. Any previous public disclosure will invalidate the application. One of the most important discoveries in recent years has been monoclonal antibodies; this is the ability of cells to produce continually one type of antibody. This has enormous potential for the pharmaceutical industry. Unfortunately the research was published in *Nature* before the patent application could be filed. As a result UK industry lost out and the technique of monoclonal antibody production has been taken up by countries all around the world. Making a patent application is a skilled job, so if you are a budding inventor always commission a professional patenting agent.

Uses

* Since a large number (millions!) of patents are held they represent an enormous and unique store of detailed and original scientific and technological information, although most science students will never need to use patent information. However, if you want to become a research scientist, or work in a science-based industry, then patents will be important and some knowledge is useful.
* Nowadays, certain scientists carry out patent analysis and study the number and type of patents in a particular area over a number of years. This often shows trends and forecasts the way an industrial research project should be planned. Keeping up-to-date with patent information is essential for many people working in commerce and industry.

Limitations

* Often detailed and difficult to understand.
* Searching through patents is a complicated business and best left to a specialist.

How to locate

Access is easy, since in 1980 the Patents Information Network was created, and certain libraries all over the UK hold copies of patent specifications. The British Library has access to over 29 million patents, and the Science Reference Information Service publishes *Patent Information News*. It is also possible to search for patents on-line.

If you are interested in patents the Patent Office provides some free pamphlets. The address to contact is:

Clerk of Stationery
Room 63
25 Southampton Buildings
London   WC2A 1AY.

Other good guides are:

Rimmer, B.M. (1988) *International Guide to Official Industrial Property Publications*, 2nd edn. BLDSC, Boston Spa.

Van Dulken, S. (1990) *Introduction to Patent Information*. Science Reference and Information Service, British Library, London.

Patents come under the term referred to as 'intellectual property', and this includes designs, copyright and trade marks. A useful book on this subject is:

Cornish, W.R. (1981) *Intellectual Property: Patents, Copyright, Trade Marks and Allied Rights*. Sweet and Maxwell, London.

Periodicals

A **periodical**, sometimes known as a journal, may be defined as a publication appearing at regular or irregular intervals, in a numbered series, and intended to be published indefinitely. Some periodicals, like *Nature*, are comprehensive covering all the sciences. Others specialize in one particular subject, for example, the *Journal of Mathematical Physics*. Periodicals are a valuable source of information and students at any level should get into the habit of reading through the range of titles available to them. Periodicals are particularly important because they contain papers which describe the new and original research being carried out in science. Also, because journals are published over a number of years, they provide a continuous record of how a particular scientific area may have evolved and developed.

Uses

* Up-to-date and original information.
* The information is specific and accurate – most periodicals have editorial boards which scrutinize the papers submitted for publication, hence the quality of the work is high

* Papers always have good reference lists.
* Some periodicals review new books and equipment, as well as carrying advertisements for products, conferences and jobs, which all helps to keep you up-to-date.
* Many journals accept short papers where exciting new developments can be speedily reported – the structure of DNA (de-oxyribonucleic acid) was first described in a letter in *Nature*.
* Papers are helpful when working out experimental details for a project.

Limitations

* Periodicals are expensive and a great many are published; most libraries only buy in a certain number.
* Access is always limited and you may have to use the ILL service.
* Many are published in foreign languages and, although some may contain English summaries, translations can prove an expensive business.

How to locate

The range of periodicals in some libraries is small and limited to general titles like *Scientific American, Nature* and *New Scientist*. These are, however, excellent reading, and well worth looking out for. Updating publications like *Current Contents* (see p. 34) are useful and will help you pick out individual papers from journals, which can then be ordered by the ILL service. Scientists rarely need a whole journal, only the papers which interest them.

Finally, if you want some idea of the vast number of periodicals which are available then consult:

Ulrich's International Periodicals Directory, 1988–89. (now including Irregular Serials and Annuals), 27th edition, 1988. Bowker; New York.

This hefty 3-volume publication gives details including title, publisher, current price, language of publication and frequency of publication. The 27th Edition also gives details of publications which are now on-line. Ulrich's can now be bought as a CD-ROM (see p. 53).

Reports

Reports are an excellent, but under-used source of information. A report is a detailed account of a particular topic, often of public concern. They are generally commissioned by government departments, associations or societies, and written on their behalf either by experts or committees. An example of a scientific report is:

The Royal Society. (1983) *The Nitrogen Cycle of the UK*. A Study Group Report. The Royal Society, London.

There are also market research reports. These are produced for industry to investigate the sales potential of a particular type of product. As much of industry is science-based, many of these reports can be useful to the science student.

Uses

* Always up-to-date, though many are prepared at great speed which can lead to occasional errors.
* Although not needed for general class work, they can prove useful for longer assignments, e.g. projects and dissertations.
* Reports are well referenced and excellent for identifying further information sources.
* Many comment upon the social, political and non-scientific issues associated with science, which will help you broaden a topic if necessary.

Limitations

* Expensive and since libraries only have a limited stock, you will probably need the ILL service.
* Market research reports are sometimes prepared, in confidence, for industry and are difficult to obtain.

How to locate

The best source to locate reports is *British Reports, Translations and Theses*. BLDSC, Boston Spa. This appears monthly and also has an annual comprehensive cumulative index. It has a subject index and each entry is given a reference number; always quote this when using the ILL service. It can also be used to trace theses and translations.

Market research reports can be traced using *Market Research: A guide to British Library Holdings* (6th edition), 1988/89, British Library Document Supply Centre, Boston Spa.

Research in progress

Subjects like genetic engineering and micro-electronics advance rapidly, and papers may be at least one year old when published. How can you discover, therefore, and comment on very recent research.

Uses

* Although not needed for general class work, it is a good idea to include some mention of recent work in projects and dissertations.

* Indicates what type of research is currently popular and attracting funding.

Limitations

* Only an outline of the work may be available, detailed experimental methods are not normally present.

How to locate

To identify current industrial research is difficult; competition from other firms and patent applications often means it is kept secret.

Work of universities, colleges and other public institutions is easier to trace. Research costs money and most of it, from the Government, is administered by various research councils. The councils have to account for their spending and publish reports, which list how the money has been distributed. Although detailed research results are not included, the reports give a good indication as to the type of work in progress. The main science research council in the UK is:

Science and Engineering Research Council
Polaris House
North Star Avenue
Swindon   SN2 1ET

The publications of this and the other research councils can be traced using the *Catalogue of British Official Publications not Published by HMSO*. Chadwyck-Healey Ltd, Cambridge. An alternative way to search out recent work is to use *Current Research in Britain* BLDSC, Boston Spa. This is published annually and is also available on-line. There are four volumes, with Volume 1 (physical sciences) and Volume 2 (biological sciences) being the most relevant. Each volume, comprehensively indexed, appears in 2 parts and is a register of research being carried out in institutes of higher education and universities.

Standards

Most things we buy, be it a power plug or can of paint, conform to what are called **standards**. In the UK they are administered by the British Standard Institution (BSI). Founded in 1901, this is an independent organization and was the first national standard body in the world. The famous BSI kite mark is often found on products. It shows the consumer that goods have been tested and produced in accordance with British Standards. There are different types of standards including size, performance, test methods, terminology and codes of practice. Many standards are useful to the scientist, for example, techniques for counting bacteria and methods for analysing chemical compounds.

Uses

* Helpful if you want to compare the efficacy of different experimental methods.
* Gives an insight into the commercial applications of science, as standards are important with society's increased use of technology.

Limitations

* Standards are subject to constant review, so always use the most recent available.

How to locate

Standards are easy to trace. The BSI publishes an annual catalogue, and the 1988 edition lists over 10 000 standards. The catalogue is also indexed. If you trace a standard which you think looks helpful you can either buy it direct from the BSI, or use one of the 250 libraries in the UK which have complete standard reference sets. A list of the libraries is in the catalogue. Standards are also available on-line, and the BSI has an enquiry service. Their address is:

BSI
Linford Wood
Milton Keynes   MK14 6LE

BSI also publishes a monthly magazine, *BSI News*, which is found in many public libraries.

There is, in addition, the National Physics Laboratory (NPL) at Teddington, Middlesex. It was founded in 1899 and operates on behalf of the Department of Trade and Industry. The NPL deals with standards of measurement, checking scientific instruments and determining physical constants. The laboratory publishes reports, which can be traced using: the *Catalogue of British Official Publications not Published by HMSO*. Chadwyck-Healey Ltd, Cambridge and *British Reports, Translations and Theses*, British Library Document Supply Centre, Boston Spa.

Statistics

Students often need to answer such questions as 'How many kidney transplant operations were carried out in Britain in 1986?' or 'What quantity of sulphuric acid has been manufactured in the UK since 1980?' when studying the applied aspects of science. Official statistics will often help. In the UK, the Central Statistics Office collects, from government departments, data on all subjects which are then published by HMSO.

Uses

* Government statistics cover a wide range of topics and can be used in many types of assignment where 'facts and figures' are needed.
* Libraries buy in many official documents, so access is not normally a problem.

Limitations

Statistics are mostly arranged in tables and figures and, although easy to follow, care is always needed in reading headings, keys and the units being used.

How to locate

HMSO produces a large number of official statistic publications. The following are particularly useful:

Guide to Official Statistics, 5th edition 1986. This details which statistics (both government and non-government) are available and where to find them. If you want to use statistics, this is the best place to start. A subject index is included.
Annual Abstract of Statistics. Appearing annually for over 100 years, this contains data on a vast number of areas. A subject index is present.
Social Trends. This appears every year and is a collection of articles, charts and diagrams describing social and economic aspects of the country.
Regional Trends. In this publication the country is divided into regions, and the statistics for each are described and compared.
Key Data. Produced for student use this presents much of the data in a condensed form. There is also a general section about using government statistics.

Other points

Some local authorities and councils produce regional statistics. These are mostly found in local libraries.

Theses

People studying for advanced qualifications, such as master's or doctorate degrees, research for a number of years in a particular area. When complete the work is written up in a special book-like form termed a **thesis**. If it is of a high enough standard, the thesis is accepted, and the qualification awarded. It is only universities and colleges like polytechnics who can grant such awards.

Uses

* Accurate and a good starting point when beginning a new specialized topic – well worth the time and effort to search them out.
* Theses are carefully vetted by a team of examiners and the quality of the work and standard of presentation is, therefore, high.
* A thesis provides an excellent source of references, together with a thorough literature review of a subject.
* Although not needed for general class work, they are helpful for projects and dissertations.

Limitations

* Very specialized in content.
* Normally only one or two copies are available for loan; academic libraries only keep their own students' work; the ILL service will be needed.
* Owing to the small number of copies, theses have a rarity value and, normally, will have to be studied in the library: they are often copied onto microfilm and special reading machines will then be needed.

How to locate

Theses are easy to trace and the best source in the UK is the *Index to Theses* The Association For Information Management (ASLIB), London. This is very easy to use and has been published since 1950. From Volume 35, completed in August 1987, the index has appeared quarterly, together with an abstract of each thesis. Each volume covers one calendar year.

Trade literature

Industry produces enormous amounts of information; leaflets describing new products, company reports, and catalogues advertising goods. Some larger companies even produce journals and magazines. Trade literature is an important source of information and historians of science, for example, can sometimes only identify old equipment by referring to a catalogue of the period.

Uses

* Trade literature shows how science and technology has changed over the years.
* Present-day literature is useful as it provides photographs and illustrations, which can be included in projects and dissertations.
* It gives an insight into how modern science is applied to various products and services.

Limitations

* Unfortunately, because of the quantity and variation in quality, much gets lost and is never saved.

How to locate

Old trade literature is difficult to find. If you need any then contact your local library. The British Library's booklet *Trade Literature in British Libraries* may also help. This library has a large collection of trade literature and the address to contact is:

Business Information Service
25 Southampton Buildings
London   WC2A 1AW

Modern trade literature is easier to get hold of; simply write a letter to the industries you think may be able to help. Advice on writing letters is given on page 85. In the author's experience most firms are extremely generous to students, and some large companies even have an education information service. However, if the whole class is working on the same topic, it may be better to nominate one person to do the writing. National firms can be traced using the following directories:

KBE (Key British Enterprises) 1989 (Britain's Top 25 British Companies. Dun and Bradstreet Ltd, London. This is published in 3 volumes: 1 and 2 contain an alphabetical listing of companies, and 3 is a reference volume providing details of company products and services, a trade and geographical index.
Kompass Register 27th edition (1989). Kompass Publishers Ltd, East Grinstead. This has 3 volumes: I lists products and services, II contains company information and III has financial data on the companies.

Local firms can be found by using the yellow pages of the local telephone directory. Some regional directories are also published and many local libraries have set up company databases. It is worth asking at your local library.

Journals like *Nature* can also be a good source of trade information. They contain advertisements for new products, which mostly give an address to write to. If a company does help then be sure to write back and say thank you. If they provide a great deal of assistance then a formal acknowledgement (see p. 103) is a good idea.

3.4 SECONDARY BOOK SOURCES

Secondary book sources include bibliographies, current awareness publications, newspapers and press clippings, reference books, reviews, textbooks and translations.

Bibliographies

A **bibliography** is a list of references, and for each one, full details are given, such as author(s), title, date of publication and publisher. Some commercial bibliographies include size of book, number of pages and current price. All good scientific writing contains a bibliography and page 113 describes how to construct one for your own work. Since the most difficult part of any information search is getting started, a bibliography, correctly used, is a good place to begin. Once you have found a few relevant books and articles, they will contain lists of references which will, in turn, lead on to other sources. Bibliographies are also termed reference lists, literature cited or other similar term.

Uses

* Helpful for checking details for an ILL request, or when preparing a bibliography of your own, *British Books in Print* (*BBIP*) was used to check the bibliography of this book.
* *BBIP* and similar publications have a subject index system which is useful to identify references when beginning a new topic.
* Commercial bibliographies are readily available: most libraries have at least one – they need them to catalogue their books! Science students do not use them enough.

Limitations

* Commercial bibliographies only list books and similar material. Individual scientific papers and periodicals are not included.

How to locate

Three well known examples follow.

British National Bibliography. British Library, London. This appears weekly, with monthly, four monthly, annual and some larger cumulated indexes. The main part of every issue is arranged by the Dewey Decimal Classification (see p. 60), together with author, title and subject index.

British Books in Print (BBIP). Whitaker, London. This appears annually and is updated monthly on microfiche. Although published for the book trade, it is very useful for the student, and as its name suggests gives details of every book currently available in the UK. A copy is in nearly every library and a CD-ROM version is now available (see p. 53).

Bibliographic Index: a cumulative bibliography of bibliographies. H.W. Wilson Co., New York. This appears half-yearly, with an annual cumulation. It is an excellent information source.

Other notes

The Science Reference Library (see p. 68) also compiles bibliographies (called guidelines) on selected scientific subjects. You can always write and enquire if they have one you need.

Current awareness publications

Scientific information is published in enormous quantities in many books, reports and periodicals etc. Even if you could afford to buy every one, you would not have enough time to read them. How do scientists, therefore, keep up with new developments? Current awareness publications help solve the problem. Certain publishers go through all the recent periodicals, theses, conference proceedings, books and sometimes patents etc., extracting from them details of contents which are then indexed and arranged in various ways and finally published. If you have access to any current awareness titles, be sure to use them; they are an excellent source of information.

Uses

* Useful for searching out relatively new information about a subject: the cumulative indexes are particularly helpful.
* Author indexes help locate the work of a particular scientist.
* Very useful in project work where recent knowledge about experimental methods may be needed.
* Although most current awareness journals are cumbersome and heavy with very small print, don't be put off. All have 'how to use' sections and

with a little practice they can provide a wealth of information. Some are now produced on CD-ROM (see p. 53) which are much easier to use.

Limitations

Only bibliographical details of references may be given, and you will, therefore, need to use the ILL service. Abstracts give more information, which is sometimes sufficient depending on your needs. Although relatively up-to-date it takes time to produce a current awareness publication because of the abstracting, indexing and publication processes involved. There is, therefore, a delay between the appearance of a research paper in a journal and its mention in a current awareness title.

Current awareness publications are very expensive and only large libraries subscribe to them. Nowadays many are on-line and, therefore, may be available at more libraries.

How to locate

The following examples of current awareness publications are very well known and particularly useful to scientists.

Current contents

This is published weekly by the Institute for Scientific Information, Philadelphia, USA. It contains reproductions of the contents pages of the latest journals in a particular field. Each issue contains an author and subject index. The subject index (called the Title Word index) is made up from the significant keywords from every title of each paper listed in one issue. *Current Contents* is published in a number of subjects, and those used by scientists include: *Current Contents: Agriculture, Biology and Environmental Sciences; Current Contents: Engineering, Technology and Applied Sciences; Current Contents: Life Sciences;* and *Current Contents: Physical, Chemical and Earth Sciences. Current Contents* is now available on disc for use with computers.

Indexes

These provide full bibliographical details of papers and other information sources. Those most helpful are as follows.

British Humanities Index. This is published by the Library Association, London, and indexes articles in British newspapers and journals. Don't let the title put you off using this index; it has some excellent references to general scientific articles. It is published quarterly, with annual cumulations.

Current Technology Index (CTI). This is also published by the Library Association and until 1980 appeared as the British Technology Index. It is issued monthly, with an annual cumulative index, and is a guide to articles about science and technology which appear only in British technical journals (over 350). All branches of science and technology are covered and it is useful for their industrial applications. Although certain subjects like medicine and agriculture are not included, related topics like the chemistry and industrial production of drugs and agrochemicals are. An author and subject index are present. *CTI* is now available on-line through the *DIALOG* system.

Science Citation Index (SCI). This is also published by the Institute of Scientific Information. It appears bi-monthly, with an annual cumulation, and includes science, medicine, agriculture, technology and the behavioural sciences. *SCI* covers over 3000 journals and in addition to indexing every paper by author and subject, also indexes every reference which is mentioned in the text, footnotes, and reference list of each paper. As a result *SCI* is comprehensively indexed in four ways.

First, the *Source Index*, which is the complete author index, alphabetically arranged, together with a full bibliographic record of all articles published under a particular name.

Secondly, the *'Permuterm' subject index*, which is a very detailed index, with each significant word in a title linked with every other significant word. If you have a vague idea about a subject this index can be used to search out any relevant articles.

Thirdly, the *Citation Index*, which lists every author, together with full bibliographical details which have been cited by another author in a paper. Details of the citing author and publication are also given. Although this index is more complex, it can help in a number of ways. For example, it can assist in compiling a working reference list for a subject, or check if a named scientist is researching in a certain area.

Finally, the *Corporate Index*, which identifies all publications from a single institution, or from individual scientists in a particular institution.

SCI is a somewhat complicated current awareness journal and the instructions need careful reading. It is, however, a very versatile aid to information retrieval and worth the effort. It is now available on-line and as a CD-ROM (see p. 53).

Abstracts

Abstracts, in addition to giving full bibliographical details, provide a short paragraph or abstract about the contents of each reference. There are a number of abstracting publications on the market and are worth using if available. The important scientific publications are listed here.

Physics Abstracts, published twice monthly by the Institution of Electrical Engineers (INSPEC). The abstracts cover the whole field of physics, and there is an easy-to-use guide on the front cover of each edition. There is also a detailed classification and contents section. The numbers given in the subject guide refer to the classification scheme and not to the abstracts themselves. The abstracts are also indexed by author's name. Cumulative indexes (subject and author) appear twice a year.

Chemical Abstracts, prepared by the Chemical Abstracting Service and published by the American Chemical Society, USA. The abstracts appear weekly and cover the whole range of chemical literature. All entries are indexed in three ways. There is first *The Keyword Index*, which uses significant words and phrases from the title and text from each paper. It can also be used as a subject index. Secondly, in *The Author Index*, author's and co-author's surnames are arranged alphabetically. Thirdly, *The Patent Index* in which the patent numbers are arranged consecutively, and organized by the code of the country granting the patent.

The instructions on how to use *Chemical Abstracts* only appear in the first issue of every year (early January). Although relatively easy to follow they need careful reading. Cumulative indexes for the abstracts are produced at six-monthly intervals and indexed according to author, general subject, chemical substance, formula and patent (containing a ring system index).

Biological Abstracts, published monthly by Biosis, USA. The abstracts are indexed four ways: first the *Author Index,* arranged as in *Chemical Abstracts* described above. Secondly, the *Biosystematic Index.* This separates each abstract by taxonomic category (phylum, class, order and family). It is useful for searching out references on a particular group of organisms. Thirdly, there is the *Generic Index.* If a generic or genus and species name appears in any of the abstracts this is also indexed. It saves time if you want information about a particular named organism. Finally, the *Subject Index,* which, like *Chemical Abstracts,* uses significant words and phrases appearing in the title or content of an abstract.

Cumulative indexes, using the same categories as above, appear every six months. Up to the end of 1984 an extra index called the '*Concept Index*' was included. This categorized each item under broad subject headings like 'endocrine system' and 'reproduction'. In the current *Biological Abstracts* these general terms can be found in the subject index. Every issue contains instructions on how to use the abstracts.

Newspapers and press clippings

Many science students fail to realize that newspapers are a valuable source of scientific information. Nowadays many newspapers (e.g. *The Guardian*) have special issues and supplements devoted to subjects like the environment and computing.

Uses

* Newspapers are worth searching through if you need information about the controversial issues of science such as toxic waste or nuclear energy. They also provide an insight into the public and political opinion at the time.

Limitations

* Newspapers are produced at great speed so check the accuracy of any story. Further, even the quality newspapers often misspell scientific words: again check carefully.

How to locate

Searching through papers is a tedious business and fortunately indexes are produced to shorten the process.

In the UK the indexes to *The Times* and *The Financial Times* are the best and most comprehensive. They are also easy to find since nearly every public library takes the papers, together with their annual indexes. Indexes for both papers are extremely easy to use and provide full details including date of newspaper, page and column number.

The Times index has been published since 1906, and from 1973 also includes *The Sunday Times, The Times Literary Supplement, The Times Education Supplement* and *The Times Higher Educational Supplement*.

If you need to consult newspapers it is worth asking at your local newspaper offices. They normally keep old editions and often compile an index of regional issues.

For the real enthusiast the reference section of the British Library has one of the largest newspaper collections in the world, with over 35 000 different titles in its catalogue.

Press clippings

Some libraries search local and national newspapers to compile a press clippings (or cuttings) collection. These tend to be about regional issues and local events. Press clippings may be useful and it is worth checking to see what is available. If you do use a collection always try to check the source of each clipping, to verify its date of publication and authenticity. A press clipping bureau can be employed to do this for you. They are, however, expensive and normally used by show business people and the like to monitor coverage in the press.

Reference books

At some point you will need to use a reference book. Different types of scientific reference books are available and a number are described below.

Uses

* They are a good starting point when searching out material on an unfamiliar topic, or seeking a specific piece of information such as a chemical name or formula. Also, most reference books list their information sources. This can be useful in providing additional references on a topic. Many books have their entries cross-referenced; this also helps in locating new sources of information.

Limitations

* The information may be out-of-date, especially in science where new discoveries are being made all the time – always use the latest edition possible.

* With so many types of reference books on the market the level and quality varies – always read a number to get a balanced view on any subject you are researching.

How to locate

Most libraries have a good selection, so access is not a problem. An excellent general guide to reference material is:

Walford, A.J. (ed.) (1980) *Walford's Guide to Reference Material. Vol: Science and Technology*, 4th edition. The Library Association, London.

Examples of reference books used by scientists

Encyclopaedias

A large number are available. They may be either general, covering all knowledge, or subject-specific. A particular advantage of encyclopaedias is that many are written for the layman and are easy to understand. This is helpful when beginning a new topic. Two examples of useful encyclopaedias are:

The New Encyclopaedia Britannica (16th edition, 1988). Encyclopaedia Britannica Inc., Chicago.

McGraw-Hill Encyclopedia of Science and Technology (6th edition, 1987). McGraw-Hill, New York.

Dictionaries

Dictionaries provide definitions and explanations of terms and phrases. Like encyclopaedias they may be either comprehensive, (for example, *The Oxford English Dictionary*), or subject-based. A number of excellent scientific dictionaries are available. The Penguin range and the Collins Dictionary series are especially good for students.

Handbooks

These are sometimes called companions, and are used for looking up specific information like chemical formulae, constants such as boiling points, and units of measurement. A very large number are published, for example:

CRC Handbook of Chemistry and Physics: A ready reference book of chemical and physical data (1986). Chemical Rubber Co., Cleveland, Ohio.

Directories

These provide names and addresses. In addition to the well known telephone directory and its yellow pages, there are a number of specialized titles which are useful to the scientist. Always try and double-check the address of any organization, person, etc. you wish to contact. This can be done by using the appropriate regional telephone directory (most post offices have copies). Other useful examples are:

Adkins, R.T. (ed.) (1988) *Guide to Government Departments and other libraries*. Science Reference and Information Service, British Library, London. This lists specialized libraries found in the UK (see p. 68).

Burkitt, J. (1979) *Directory of Scientific Directories. A World Guide to Scientific Directories including medicine, agriculture, engineering manufacturing and industrial directories* (3rd edition). Hodgson, Harlow.

The books listed under 'Government, official and general organizations' on page 51 are also directories.

Year books
As the name implies these books set out to provide updated information and give a survey of events, or record of research work carried out during the year. Like any reference book they may be broad-based or subject-specific in content. Examples of year books include:

Whitaker's Almanack 1989 (121st edition). Whitaker & Sons Ltd, London.

Year Book of Science and Technology. McGraw-Hill, London.

The books listed under 'Universities etc.' on page 51 are also year books.

Other points about reference books

Reference books have their contents compiled and arranged in different ways. Fortunately most provide 'How to use' sections: read these carefully before you begin a search.

Libraries often keep all the reference books, irrespective of subject, in one section. Know where this is in your main study library. Reference books are not usually allowed out on loan and are always available for use.

Reviews

Certain scientific papers are called reviews. A **review**, as its name suggests, recalls the changes which have taken place over a number of years in some aspect of science. An author writing a review must first sift through all the literature and current information. The final paper should not be a mere chronological summary, but a balanced account, where the discoveries and trends are both identified and discussed.

Although reviews are secondary publications relying on previously published work, they sometimes appear in primary journals. Don't confuse this type of academic review with criticisms of films, plays, records and books which are also called reviews.

Uses

* They provide a relatively up-to-date account of a subject.
* Contain long and comprehensive reference lists.
* Often describe industrial applications.
* Provide a good starting point when beginning a new subject.

Limitations

* Some may be biased and reflect the views of the author.
* Availability is limited, and the ILL service may be needed.

How to locate

Reviews appear in journals with titles like *Advances in Analytical Chemistry and Instrumentation* and *Annual Review of Physical Chemistry*. See what is locally available.

The main publication to search out review titles is: *Current Serials Received* (British Library Document Supply Centre & Science Reference and Information Service, Boston Spa). This book appears each year in April.

Textbooks

Students are often recommended to use one main book for the whole of their course. This type of book is called a **textbook**.

Uses

* Textbooks tend to relate to one particular course and may contain much of the basic information needed for the course. As such, they are useful, for everyday class work and examination revision.

Limitations

* A textbook will not answer every query – develop the habit of 'reading around' the subject. Use all the information sources available to you, most of which have been described in this chapter.
* A large number of textbooks are published which contain much the same information. Look around and discover which is the best for you. Writing styles vary and you may find one author easier to understand. Your teacher may recommend one who is especially suited to your needs.

* Textbooks are written with a particular course in mind. If you are going to choose a book yourself then look carefully to see which market it is aimed at. As you study for more advanced qualifications you will come to rely less on textbooks as your only source of information. Start now by using the difference sources available to you.
* Although a textbook covers a number of topics, there may be subjects sparsely treated, or even omitted, which you need for your course. Go through the syllabus together with any recommended textbooks identifying these subjects. You will then need to search elsewhere for this information.
* Textbooks are being written and published all the time. Existing ones are often up-dated and new editions brought out. Keep a look out for new titles, and read the critical reviews in periodicals like *Nature* and newspapers such as *The Times Educational Supplement*. Keep an eye open for new books coming into the libraries you use.
* It takes time to write a book, so inevitably some material will be out-of-date at publication and the author may have made mistakes in collecting the information. Remember this when using a textbook.
* Although textbooks will help in everyday study, for practical work and longer assignments like essays and dissertations you will need to use a variety of different information sources.

How to locate

Most college libraries hold copies of titles recommended by teaching staff, and bookshops have a good selection at the start of the academic year in September and October. *BBIP* is a good place to search out a suitable title if you are choosing your own books.

Translations

When collecting a very large number of references, it is likely that some will be in a language you cannot understand. What do you do? In some instances the work may have already been translated. The British Library has a large collection of translated material and continually commissions translations of new research.

Uses

* May only be needed for specialized assignments.

Limitations

* Availability is always limited, although some well known books and journals are available in translation.

How to locate

The following may help you find what you need.

Journals in Translation (4th edition, 1988). BLDSC, in association with the International Translations Centre, Delft, Boston Spa. This book lists over 1000 journals which are available in English translation.
British Reports, Translations and Theses. BLDSC, London. (see p. 26).
Index Translationum: International Bibliography of Translations UNESCO, Paris. This is an annual list of translated books by country of origin, and they are classified under subject headings. It has been published since 1932.

Other points

If you are unable to find a translation, most libraries have lists of people who, for a fee, will prepare one for you. This is expensive because of the specialized scientific vocabulary involved. Before enquiring about a translation, double-check that the information cannot be obtained from an alternative source. The bibliography in the work requiring the translation is a good place to start: a similar reference in a language you can understand may be quoted.

3.5 NON-BOOK SOURCES

Non-book sources include audio-visual material, botanical gardens, culture collections, herbaria, information services, maps, microforms, museums, organisations, on-line searching and CD-ROMs, people, remote sensing information, science parks, videotex systems and zoos and nature reserves.

Audio-visual material

This includes films, videos, tapes, records, film-loops and recent developments, like inter-active video. The amount is increasing all the time, so try to keep up-to-date by looking through recent catalogues. Often audio-visual material comes with study guides and leaflets; always work through these making notes as required.

Uses

* Is extremely useful in consolidating work covered in class, but does not normally include recent research findings.
* Provides background information for essays, dissertations and projects.

* Many industries produce visual aids which provide useful illustrations of the commercial applications of science.

Limitations

* The main drawback with this type of material is that you need special equipment to use it, although many libraries have viewing and listening facilities. Most material cannot be taken out on loan.
* If you order material from commercial catalogues, there will be a hire charge, together with postage expenses. Even though some organizations loan material free of charge, postage and insurance cover will still need to be paid.

How to locate

See what is present in your local library, remembering that audio-visual material is mostly catalogued and stored separately from other stock. Certain regional directories are published. For example:

Cornish, G.P. (1988) *Directory of Audiovisual Resources in the East Midlands*. Published for the East Midland Library System by the BLDSC, Boston Spa.
Cornish, G.P. (1988) *Directory of Audiovisual Resources in Yorkshire and Humberside* (2nd edition). Published for the Yorkshire and Humberside Joint Library Services by the BLDSC, Boston Spa.

Also, the BBC and IBA produce excellent science programmes both for their education and normal services. Always check through *The Radio Times* and *TV Times* looking for useful programmes. *The Listener* magazine often carries follow-up articles on some of these programmes.

You can also consult audio-visual catalogues. Most libraries have a selection, and some are regarded as standard reference books. Those listed below are particularly good. All give full details for each entry, and include producer, distributor, title and sometimes a summary of content. The catalogues are comprehensively indexed and give details on how to obtain a particular title.

General catalogues

BUFVC Catalogue. This is the catalogue of the British University Film and Video Council which was established in 1948. The catalogue, originally available in book form, is now produced on microfiche. It contains details of material produced in British Universities, Polytechnics and Institutes of Higher Education. The material is intended for degree-level students. The entries are catalogued according to the Universal Decimal System (see p. 62) and there is an author and title index. The 1985 catalogue details over 5700 items. It is regularly updated and is on-line with the BLAISE system. The address of the Council is:

British University Film and Video Council
55 Greek Street
London   W1V 5LR.

○ *The Penguin Video Source Book* (1983) (Penguin Books, London). A well indexed book, covering a wide range of material.

Science on 16 mm Film and Video Catalogue (1985) (The Scottish Central Film Library, Glasgow). The library's address is:

The Scottish Central Film Library
74 Victoria Crescent Road
Dowanhill Road
Glasgow   G12 9JN

British Catalogue of Audio Visual Materials (1979) (The British Library: Bibliographic Services Division, London. This does not include 16 mm films, videos and musical sound recordings. The entries are arranged by the Dewey Decimal Classification System (see p. 60), and there are author, title and series indexes. Supplements were published in 1980 and 1983.

British National Film and Video Catalogue (British Film Institute, London). This appears quarterly, with a cumulative index. The non-fiction entries are classified according to the Universal Decimal System (see p. 62). The Institute's address is:

British Film Institute
21 Stephen Street
London   WC1P 1PL

Subject catalogues

* *Biology*

Maslin, D. (ed.) (1978) *Biological Sciences: a subject index of audio visual materials* (The Institute of Biology, London). The address of the Institute is:

The Institute of Biology
41 Queensbury Place
London   SW7 2ZY

* *Chemistry*

Index of Chemistry Films: A list of films, videotapes, slides, strips, loops, soundtapes, and overhead transparencies about chemistry and related topics (1984) (The Royal Society of Chemistry, London). The address of the Society is:

The Royal Society of Chemistry
Burlington House
Piccadilly
London   W1V 0BN

* *Physics*
  The Institute of Physics publishes the journal *Physics Education* which regularly reviews audio-visual material. The address of the Institute is:

  The Institute of Physics
  47 Belgrave Square
  London   SW1X 8QX

The National Sound Archive

An unusual, but important audio-visual source is The National Sound Archive. Part of the British Library, the Archive houses an enormous collection of discs (including compact discs), tape recordings and specialist videos. An ecologist may find the Archive particularly profitable, since it has over 5000 recordings of different animal sounds and noises. The Archive is open to the public, although it is advisable to contact them first, informing them of the type of recordings you would like to hear. Their address is:

The National Sound Archive
29 Exhibition Road
London   SW7 2AS

Interested users can also use the collection at the British Library Document Supply Centre, Boston Spa, West Yorkshire. Arrangements can be made by contacting the London base in the first instance. For people unable to visit either Yorkshire or London, the Archive holds *The National Register of Collections of Recorded Sound*, which provides details of recordings and similar facilities available at various organizations scattered throughout the UK. If interested, write to the Archive in London detailing your needs.

Botanical gardens

Many plants are used for food, or extracts from them included in drugs and other fine chemicals. Botanical gardens grow specimens of many economically important plants, and can provide useful information about the history and uses of particular species. The Royal Botanic Gardens at Kew are world famous for their large collections. On a smaller scale, some universities and local authorities have botanical gardens which are open to the public.

Uses

* May be useful for assignments involving the taxonomy of plants, and their economic or medicinal applications.

Limitations

* Access is a problem – it is worthwhile enquiring locally.

How to locate

The following gives details of gardens in the UK.

Henderson, D.M. (1983) *The International Directory of Botanical Gardens* (4th edition). Koeltz Scientific Books, Koenigstein.
Williams, J.T. (1974) *Plant Collections in the British Isles: A Preliminary Index*. Bentham–Moxon Trust, Kew.

Culture collections

The maintenance of organisms like bacteria and fungi in culture has always been important in the study of micro-biology. With the growing interest in biotechnology the importance of culture collections as an information source has increased on a world-wide scale. In the UK there are over 30 recognized collections of organisms such as bacteria, fungi, protozoa and algae. Many are national collections, for example, The National Collection of Industrial Bacteria. Private collections are found in universities and some larger colleges.

Uses

* For practical investigations, e.g. biotechnology, microbiology, etc.

Limitations

* Micro-organisms, even non-pathogenic forms, must always be handled using special techniques.

How to locate

Most national biological laboratory suppliers provide a range of species suited to students' needs. If you need an unusual organism then you may need a specialist collection in which case *Culture Collections* (1984) (The Science Reference Library, London). This pamphlet lists the UK collections, together with details of relevant directories, books, newsletters and information services.

The Laboratory of the Government Chemist of the Department of Trade and Industry operates a Microbial Culture Information Service (MiCIS). Their address is:

MiCIS
Laboratory of the Government Chemist
Queen's Road
Teddington
Middlesex   TW11 0LY

Herbaria

Botanists may also use dried plants in their work. A collection of dried plants is termed a **herbarium**. If a specimen has been properly prepared and well kept it can provide detailed information on the plant's anatomy and morphology. Scientists interested in plant breeding and the selection of new crops often use herbarium specimens to compare new strains with existing species. Making a herbarium was a popular Victorian pastime, and many private collections exist.

Uses

* Work involving the applied aspects of plants.
* Helpful in morphological and taxonomic studies – you may be able to observe the type specimens of a particular species.

Limitations

* Access is limited.
* Dried plants break very easily and need careful handling. Any work with herbarium material is usually well supervised.

How to locate

The Royal Botanic Gardens at Kew have a large collection, and some university botany departments still maintain a herbarium; so ask at your nearest university should you need to use one. The following books are a guide to what is available nationally.

Kent, D. H. (with the assistance of E. B. Bangerher and J. E. Lousley) (1957) *British Herbaria: An Index to the Location of Herbaria of British Vascular Plants with Biographical References to their Collectors*. Botanical Society of the British Isles, London.
Stafleu, F. A. (ed.) (1981) *Index Herbariorum: A Guide to the Location and Contents of the World's Public Herbaria*. Bohn, Scheltema and Holkema, Utrecht.

Information services

Many organizations, both private and government-sponsored, have set up information services and, usually for a fee, provide information about specialized topics, often in areas of science and technology. Industry and commerce sometimes use these facilities, rather than search out material for themselves.

Uses

* For very specialized information.

Limitations

* They tend to be expensive.

How to locate

The following directory gives details of UK information services.

Adkins, R. T. (ed.) (1988) *Guide to Government Departments and other Libraries*. Science Reference and Information Service, British Library, London.

Although the average student may never need an information service, your local library may have a special arrangement for certain subjects, so it is worth asking if anything is available. Many of the on-line agencies (see p. 51) now provide these services.

An example of a national service is the Overseas Technical Information Services (OTIS) which collates and distributes scientific and technical information collected in British Embassies all around the world. This service is sponsored by the Department of Trade and Industry and is administered by the Production Engineering Research Association (PERA). Their address is:

PERA
Melton Mowbray
Leicestershire   LE13 0PB

Maps

For certain types of work maps are very important.

Uses

* Students studying the ecology of an area may need to use maps. If the area being studied is particularly interesting then an old map may give some indication of how the region has changed.

Limitations

* Old maps may be valuable and are not always available for loan, so must be used in the library. Note that tracing from maps (if allowed) should be done carefully to avoid damage.

How to locate

In most cases the current edition of the Ordnance Survey Maps published by HMSO will be sufficient. Many public and academic libraries collect regional maps and have special map collections, so a local inquiry could prove worthwhile. Map collections are usually classified according to geographical area and often have a separate catalogue from other library stock.

Microforms

These are miniature photographic negatives of the printed page. Three types are available, namely microfilm, microfiche and microcard. Many bibliographies, indexes, catalogues and abstracts etc. are now prepared both in micro and book form. The advantages to a library are that microform takes up less space than books.

Uses

* It is possible to see old and rare books on microfilm, which otherwise would be difficult to obtain.
* Many ILL requests, especially theses, are now sent as microforms.

Limitations

* The main drawback for the reader is that special reading machines are needed which become tiring for the eyes over long periods, although some machines have built in photocopying facilities. The need for special machines obviously means that the material must be used in the library; it cannot be taken home.

How to locate

Every library has different quantities of microform material which is often catalogued and stored separately from other stock.

Many publications now appear in microform and a good guide is the *Guide to Microforms in Print (1985)* (Meckler Publishing, London). There are 2 volumes giving details of authors and titles. A companion volume is also published as a subject guide.

Museums

Museums range from the very large, for example the Science Museum, South Kensington, London, to small and specialized collections.

Uses

* Excellent places to visit if you want to discover how science and technology has changed, and been applied over the years.
* Postcards and leaflets on sale can always be used in projects and dissertations.

* Some museums have an education service which may be able to help, if you have an inquiry.

Limitations

* Museums tend not to have all their stock on display at the same time, so it is best to contact the curator if you need to make a visit.

How to locate

See what is present locally: there are two guides which list all the museums in the UK.

Museums Yearbook, including a directory of Museums and Galleries of the British Isles. The Museum Association, London. This appears every year and is very comprehensive. Within the association there are two specialist groups concerned with science: the Biology Curators' Group; and the Group for Scientific, Technological and Medical Collections. The address of the Association is:

The Museum Association
34 Bloomsbury Way
London   WC1A 2SF

Hudson, K. and Nicholls, A. (1987) *The Cambridge Guide to the Museums of Britain and Ireland.* Cambridge University Press, Cambridge. This is an excellent guide and contains a useful subject index.

Organizations

Organizations like Trade Associations provide a wealth of useful information. Many have educational departments and are very willing to send out material.

Uses

* Many courses now expect students to look at the broader aspects of science. When preparing this type of work it is sometimes a good idea to contact the relevant industry and/or professional organization to seek their opinion. Many produce useful information, giving details of products and services.

Limitations

* Access is not straightforward and you may have to write in the first instance. Be polite, following the advice on page 85.

How to locate

Several good directories are available and the following are particularly useful.

Government, official and general organizations
Codlin, E. M. (ed.) (1982) *ASLIB Directory of Information Sources in the United Kingdom. Volume 1. Science, Technology and Commerce* (5th edition). ASLIB, London. This gives an alphabetical list of names, organizations, libraries and trade associations etc. A good subject index is included.

Sellar, L. (ed.) (1989) *Councils, Committees and Boards: A handbook of advisory, consultative, executive and similar bodies in British Public Life* (7th edition). CBD Research Ltd, Beckenham. This handbook gives details of research councils and various scientific organizations like The Royal Society.

Henderson, G. P. and Henderson, S. P. A. (1988) *Directory of British Associations and Associations in Ireland* (9th edition). CBD Research Ltd, Beckenham. This covers nearly every association and subject you can think about. There is an excellent index.

Universities, colleges and anything educational
Education Year Book (1990). Longman, Harlow.
The World of Learning (1990). Europa Publications Ltd, London.

Both books are comprehensive guides to universities, schools and colleges.

Industries and industrial organizations
Use the sources given under Trade literature on page 30.

On-line searching and CD-ROMs

Computer databases are now being used to store bibliographical details of books, periodicals, patents, in fact every type of information. There are databases on many subjects, with science and technology having the largest number. Using a specialized computer terminal, the public telephone system and a modem (a device which links computers via the telephone) it is possible to link up with a database and access its information. This is called **on-line searching**. The bases are run as businesses and there is a charge for their services. As the telephone system is used, the bases can be anywhere in the world. Two well-known systems are:

BLAISE (British Library Automated Information Service). This database is in the UK and contains details of over 2 000 000 books published in the UK and US.
ORBIT (On-line Retrieval of Bibliographic Information). This is owned by the System Development Corporation in California, and has a large number of databases.

At the end of your search you can either have the replies immediately and read them off the computer terminal screen, or have them printed at the databases and posted on later.

Uses

* Can obtain references, including recent work, covering a particular subject, from a wide variety of sources.
* May be used to answer specific queries.
* Data can be accessed speedily at any time, day or night.
* Accurate and up-to-date.
* Very reliable searching, as computers, unlike people, do not become bored, and their concentration never wavers.
* Many well-known journals, indexes and abstracts are now available on-line.
* You can search out several related areas of knowledge at the same time, and the search terms can be changed quickly if no useful references are being found.

Limitations

* Using a commercial database is expensive. There is a subscription fee to the database, the cost of the telephone call (often to the other side of the world) and the cost of each individual search. This type of searching only informs you of what is available and provides bibliographical details; you may still need the ILL service.
* A definite idea of the type of information needed is required, since it is difficult to browse through a database as you would a library catalogue.
* You will need specialist advice to help with the search.
* You need to select the right database; many are limited to specialized areas and only have records for a number of years.

How to search on-line

Many libraries have an on-line facility and, because it is so fast and accurate, hopefully it will become cheaper and even more widely available. Provided you can afford it, and have the right equipment and software, there is no reason why you cannot search on-line using a home computer. In order to search effectively you must have a fixed idea as to the area you wish to access.

An example of on-line searching
Suppose you are preparing an assignment on food additives and wish to search a suitable database using 'food additives' as your search term (this is sometimes called a 'key word'). The reply would most likely run into thousands of references and prove too expensive to be printed. In this case you would need to redefine your search term, for example to one specific type of additive, such as a colour or preservative. It may even be more practical to limit your search over a fixed number of years.

A particular advantage with computer searching is that several search terms can be linked together at the same time. With the above example, colours could be joined with one type of food and/or some other aspect of additives (e.g. health, biochemistry, mode of action, side effects, industrial use).

An important point not to be overlooked with this type of searching is that although a great deal of time will be saved in locating material, it still needs to be read and studied. Computers cannot do all the work!

CD-ROMs

CD-ROM stands for compact disc read-only memory, and is a very recent method used to store and retrieve information. The discs look like ordinary music compact discs, but instead of sound they store text, pictures, graphs – in fact just about anything. Very large amounts of information may be stored on one disc, somewhere in the region of 250 000 pages of text. CD-ROM searching is similar to on-line methods in that a computer is used. In addition, a CD-ROM disc drive and special software is needed. The equipment is highly expensive and only found in large libraries. Unlike on-line searching, because the data is on the disc, the computer terminal does not link up with a distant database. For the reader this means more time is available, so it is possible to browse and go back to research a subject as many times as are needed.

To date only a limited number of discs are published. Hopefully, they will become cheaper and more available, since using CD-ROMs is one of the easiest ways to trace information. The following guides list most of the current titles:

Cormack, E. (1988) *The CD-ROM Directory, 1989* (3rd edition). TFPL, London.
Desmarais, N. (ed.) (1990) *CD-Roms in Print 1990*. Meckler Ltd, London.
Emard, J. P. (ed.) (1988) *CD-Roms in Print 1988–1989. An International Guide*. Meckler Ltd, London.

People

People are a very important source of information. Sometimes scientists visit local universities, colleges and societies to give lectures on their work, and often these are open to the public.

People nearer home can also offer advice. If you have a relative or friend who knows about something scientific, why not enlist their help if you need it? They may help you sort out and understand points you find difficult.

Uses:

* Helpful for assignments about the lives of famous scientists.
* You obtain a personal, sometimes anecdotal, view of science.
* The work described in a speech may be very recent and not yet published.

Limitations:

* Personal views are sometimes heavily biased.
* Access to some people is difficult.

How to locate

For public lectures, be aware of what is happening in your area. Read your local newspaper for advertisements, and watch out for notices in public libraries. Some local authorities publish regular guides of forthcoming events.

Try to go to as many relevant lectures as possible, and remember to make notes of what is said. Take a firm pad of paper to write on – balancing a sheet of paper on your knee is a difficult business!

Alternatively you may wish to contact a scientist directly by letter. Tracing someone is not always easy. A paper written by them may sometimes contain their address. Using *Abstracts* and *SCI* will identify a recent publication. For well-known scientists the following publications are also useful:

Who's Who A. & C. Black, London. The 141st edition published in 1989 contains more than 28 000 entries.
Who's Who of British Scientists 1980/81 (1980) Simon Books, Dorking.
American Men and Women of Science. Cumulative Index of editions 1-14 (1983) Bowker, New York.
Who's Who in Science in Europe (1984) Longman, London.

If you can obtain an address then always be polite when you write (see page 85). Many people lead busy lives, so expect some delay before you receive a reply. Usually, scientists do their best to help a genuine inquiry, recalling the time when they were students. Be prepared, however, for those who will ignore your letter, and above all never pester.

Remote sensing information

Techniques such as X-rays, aerial photography and ultrasound are termed **remote sensing**, and all provide useful information for the scientist. In recent years the most spectacular advance has been information which is gathered from satellites orbiting around the earth. The data is analysed in a number of ways, for example, in weather forecasting. Other important applications include monitoring the earth's resources, such as the location of mineral deposits, and crop and timber production. Satellite information can also be used for the early detection of pests and diseases such as the desert locust. The use of satellites is an exciting area, and it is worth being aware of new developments.

Uses

* Remote sensing will only be needed for specialized work.

Limitations

* Special equipment is needed to interpret the data.

How to locate

A useful book is:

Curran, P. J. (1985) *Principles of Remote Sensing*. Longman, London.

Resource material may be obtained from:

National Remote Sensing Centre
Space Department, Room 238
Aircraft Establishment
Farnborough   GU14 6TD

Focal Point Audio-Visual Ltd
251 Copnor Road
Portsmouth   PO3 5EE

Carnegie Laboratory of Physics
University of Dundee
Dundee   DD1 4HN

Science parks

Many universities now have science parks. A **science park** is a group of buildings on the campus to encourage links between academic research and industry. Science parks are also called innovation centres and technology development units.

Uses

* Helpful when studying the commercial applications of science.
* They are concerned with the transfer of research ideas into new products and services.

Limitations

* Some of their activity may be very specialized and confidential.

How to locate

It may be worth contacting the park nearest to you when studying the industrial applications of science. In recent years science parks have attracted a great deal of interest, and there is a lot of information about them. The contact address is:

UK Science Park Association
44 Four Oaks Road
Sutton Coldfield
West Midlands   B74 2TL.

Videotex systems

It is now possible to access information in your own home using the television set. Such systems are called **videotex** and two types exist: Teletext, and Viewdata.

Teletext

This began in the UK in 1976, and, at present, there is ORACLE (Optional Reception of Announcements by Coded Line Electronics) operated by the IBA (Independent Broadcasting Authority), and CEEFAX (See Facts) of the BBC (British Broadcasting Corporation).

Viewers call up on their TV screens pages of information instead of the normal programmes. The Teletext data is transmitted along with the programmes, and a specially modified TV set decodes the signal and displays the information on the screen. The Teletext is controlled by a keypad unit which looks like a pocket calculator.

Viewdata

This system also uses a modified TV set, except the signals are sent along the telephone line and not transmitted with normal programmes. As with Teletext the viewer has a keypad to call up the information. As the telephone line is used there is more interaction with the viewer, who can send messages back down the telephone line to the computer which stores the information. In the UK PRESTEL is the main viewdata system. It was developed by British Telecom and was the first of its kind in the world. PRESTEL has access to over 200 000 pages of information, and organizations like publishers, government departments and catalogue companies rent computer space and supply the data. They are termed 'information providers'. PRESTEL is more expensive than either CEEFAX or ORACLE, since in addition to the cost of the specially adapted TV set there are telephone charges, a standing charge to PRESTEL and sometimes even page charges, depending which information is being looked at.

Uses

* Information is available in your home. It is quick and easy to access.

Limitations

* At the moment most of the information on videotex is current affairs, news bulletins and advertising. Little is of direct use to the scientist, although PRESTEL does have an education service. As more people use these systems the amount of material available will increase, and, in the future, they may be an important source of scientific information with whole libraries 'on-call' in your sitting room.

How to locate

Many television sets are fitted with Teletext systems and a number of libraries have PRESTEL – ask locally.

Zoos and nature reserves

Zoos, wildlife centres and nature reserves are all very important information sources for the biologist.

Uses:

* For any work on the behaviour of animals such as feeding habits, or locomotion, where observation of the living organism is needed.
* Many have an education information service and can give lots of assistance.

Limitations:

* Most zoos and reserves are run as businesses and admission charges can prove expensive.
* You may be limited to the type of work you can do.

How to locate

In addition to local zoos and reserves the National Federation of Zoological Garden supplies, on receipt of a stamped addressed envelope, a list of their

UK members. The address to write to is:

The National Federation of Zoological Gardens of Great Britain and Ireland
Zoological Gardens
Regent's Park
London   NW1 4RY

Finally don't just turn up and expect everything to be available – always write beforehand.

SUMMARY

This chapter focuses on the various sources of information available to the science student.
  The key points are:

- realize that information is either new and original (primary) or second-hand (secondary)
- note that information may be in both book and non-book form
- be aware that information comes in many different sources and their number is increasing all the time
- list all the different sources present in the libraries near you, and learn how to use them
- know the uses and limitations of the sources you use
- use a number of different sources the next time you begin an assignment
- don't be dependent on one source (usually a textbook) – get a balanced view.

4

Locating scientific information: using libraries

Chapter 3 outlines the different information sources available to the scientist, many of which are found in libraries. This chapter examines the ways libraries classify and catalogue scientific information, and describes some of the other services they provide. To help you get maximum benefit from a library, a user's check list is also included.

The topics covered in this chapter include:

- classification and cataloguing
- classification systems
- library catalogues
- specialized library services
- a user's check list.

4.1 CLASSIFICATION AND CATALOGUING

All libraries, even small ones, need to organize and keep an accurate record of books, periodicals and other material. The system used to separate stock into different subject areas is termed classification.

Bibliographical records are kept for every item, and these make up a library's catalogue. This is the complete list of everything in stock. Correctly used, the catalogue will enable you to find the whereabouts of any item, and show you what is available on a particular subject.

A basic understanding of the common library classification and cataloguing systems will help you to search out scientific information quickly and efficiently. On first reading, some of the different methods may appear complicated. In fact, they are straightforward; you only have to sort alphabetically and numerically.

Having read this chapter, the best advice is to go to all the libraries you are likely to use and practise using their classification and cataloguing methods.

4.2 CLASSIFICATION SYSTEMS

All library classification systems divide knowledge into major areas, which are, in turn, sub-divided several times so that all items on the same subject are placed together. Librarians use symbols, termed a notation, to represent each subject. The symbols, usually a combination of numbers and/or letters for each subject, are called the classmark. This is normally written, for example with a book, on the spine as well as inside the cover. Classmarks help with shelving and storage; they ensure that each item is in its correct place, so it can be found when needed.

Three well known classification systems are: The Dewey Decimal System, The Library of Congress System, and The Universal Decimal System. Each system is briefly described, together with the outline classification for science.

The Dewey Decimal System (also known as the Dewey, DC and DDC system)

Originally devised by Melvil Dewey (1851–1931), this is now used worldwide and is found in many public and academic libraries. The system divides knowledge into 10 classes.

000 – Generalities
100 – Philosophy and related disciplines
200 – Religion
300 – Social sciences
400 – Language
500 – Pure sciences
600 – Technology (applied sciences)
700 – The arts and recreation
800 – Literature
900 – General geography and history and their auxiliaries

Each class is then separated into ten divisions numbering 0–9. Division 0 being used for general works and 1–9 for the different subjects within a major area. For example, Pure science is split as follows.

500 – General works of pure science
510 – Mathematics
520 – Astronomy and allied sciences
530 – Physics
540 – Chemistry and allied sciences
550 – Earth sciences (e.g. geology) and allied subjects
560 – Palaeontology
570 – Life sciences
580 – Botany
590 – Zoology

Technology (applied sciences) at 600 is similarly divided.

600 – General works of technology
610 – Medicine
620 – Engineering and allied subjects   and so on...

Each division is further divided into 10 sections. For example, physics at 530 is divided as follows.

530 – General works of physics
531 – Mechanics, general
532 – Mechanics of fluids
533 – Mechanics of gases
534 – Sound and related vibrations
535 – Visible light (optics) and paraphotic phenomena
536 – Heat
537 – Electricity and electronics
538 – Magnetism
539 – Modern physics (molecular, atomic and nuclear physics)

The Dewey system permits further sub-divisions to any degree with the addition of decimal notation. For example:

535.3 – Transmission, absorption, emission of visible light
535.33 – Optical instruments
535.332 – Microscopes
535.332 2 – Simple microscopes
535.332 3 – Compound microscopes
535.332 4 – Ultramicroscopes
535.332 5 – Electron microscopes

The Library of Congress System

This was devised by Dr H. Putman in 1897 for the library of the United States Congress in Washington, DC. Many universities around the world use this system.

Knowledge is split into divisions, or fields, indicated by 21 letters of the alphabet. The scheme is as follows:

A – General works
B – Philosophy, religion
C – Auxiliary sciences of history
D – History, general and Old World
E – America
F – America
G – Geography, anthropology, recreation
H – Social sciences, economics, sociology
J – Political science
K – Law

L – Education
M – Music
N – Fine arts
P – Language and literature
Q – Science
R – Medicine
S – Agriculture
T – Technology
U – Military science
V – Naval science
Z – Bibliography and library service

A second letter shows the subject areas within a field. For example, science at Q is split as follows.

Q – General science
QA – Mathematics (including computer science)
QB – Astronomy
QC – Physics
QD – Chemistry
QE – Geology
QH – Natural history
QK – Botany
QL – Zoology
QM – Human anatomy
QP – Physiology and biochemistry
QR – Microbiology

The letters are followed by numbers which indicate special topics within a subject, so that QH 541 refers to ecology, and QD 151 to physical organic chemistry. For more specialized subjects, additional decimal points followed by letters and numbers are added to the classmark.

The Universal Decimal System (also known as the UDC system)

This system, based on the Dewey system, is found in many industrial and technological libraries. It is published and kept up-to-date by the BSI. Knowledge is divided into 10 areas, each represented by a single number as follows.

0 – Generalities
1 – Philosophy, psychology
2 – Religion, theology
3 – Social sciences (includes statistics, law and education)
4 – Philology, languages
5 – Pure science: mathematical and natural
6 – Applied science: medicine and technology
7 – Arts (includes architecture, photography, entertainment and sport)
8 – Literature
9 – Geography, biography and history

Each area is then divided into 10 parts, and science is arranged thus:

5 – Mathematics and natural science
51 – Mathematics
52 – Astronomy, geodesy and surveying
53 – Physics and mechanics
54 – Chemistry
55 – Geology and associated sciences, meteorology
56 – Palaeontology, fossils
57 – Biological sciences
58 – Botany, plant biology and taxonomy
59 – Zoology, animal biology and taxonomy

The notation is built up by adding both numbers, using the decimal system, and signs (e.g. + / :). The decimal points divide at three-digit intervals to make up the final classmark (e.g. Radar 621.396.96). The UDC is a detailed classification scheme and allows for many discrete areas of specialized knowledge. For this reason it is mostly used in libraries which cover a narrow subject area.

Additional points about classification

○ Reference books are usually included under Generalities.
○ In academic libraries fiction is classified under Literature. Public libraries normally keep it separate from non-fiction and classify either by author, or type of novel (e.g., western, romance, horror).
○ Other classification methods exist (e.g., the Bliss Bibliographic Scheme) and some libraries either invent their own, or adapt the well known systems for their particular needs. Always check the first time you use a library.

4.3 LIBRARY CATALOGUES

How do the different classification schemes work in practice? For every item in a library there is a full bibliographical record. These are stored in various ways, for example, on cards, microfiche, or computer database, and together make up the library's catalogue. This is arranged in several ways depending upon the needs of the library. Most libraries have an author catalogue, a subject index and a subject catalogue.

Author catalogue

This has a record for each item, arranged alphabetically according to author's name. The author might be the surname of an editor or writer (e.g. Dickens, Charles) the name of a society (e.g. The Royal Society),

Government Department (e.g. Department of Education and Science) or institution (e.g. Oxford University). Sometimes there may be more than one entry for a piece of work. For example, if a book has two authors (e.g. Jones, D.T. and Evans, C.E.), or is about a famous person (e.g. Albert Einstein) there will be an entry for each name associated with the item. A report would be entered under the name of the organization which produced it. Some reports are better known by a particular person involved with its production and in such instances there will be a second entry in that name.

If the library has several copies of an item, there may be separate entries for each copy, or a single entry informing how many copies are available. Each record will also give the classmark, the location in the library, whether the item may be taken out on loan, or is part of the reference collection. Figure 4.1(a) is an example of an author entry as it might appear on a card index when classified according to the Dewey system.

Periodicals are always listed alphabetically in the author catalogue, either according to their name (e.g. *Nature* would be under 'N') or the society responsible for the publication (e.g. the *Journal of the American Chemical Society* would be under 'J' and also 'A'). To save time searching in the main author catalogue most libraries keep a separate list, or catalogue, for their periodical holdings. Although the titles of periodicals and the organizations which produce them will be catalogued, the names of individual authors for the scientific papers contained in each periodical will not be included.

Uses of the author catalogue

* If you need to know what items have been written by, or about, a particular person.
* In tracing an item when only the author's name is known.
* To check publication details when compiling a bibliography.

Subject index

This is an alphabetical list of all the subjects present in a library's stock. Against each subject will be the classmark, according to the classification system being used. If a library uses the Dewey method, part of the index might read as follows.

Physics – electricity   537
Physics – electromagnetic spectrum   539.2
Physics – electromagnetism   537
Physics – electron   537.56
Physics – electronic circuits   537.535 3

4.1a: An author entry

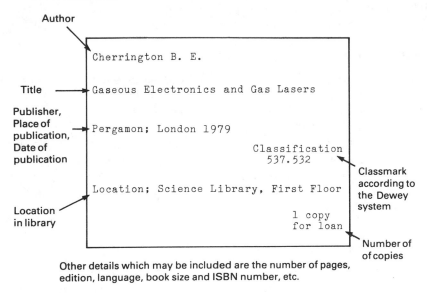

Author

Cherrington B. E.

Title ⟶ Gaseous Electronics and Gas Lasers

Publisher,
Place of
publication,
Date of
publication ⟶ Pergamon; London 1979

Classification
537.532

Classmark
according to
the Dewey
system

Location; Science Library, First Floor

Location
in library

1 copy
for loan

Number of
of copies

Other details which may be included are the number of pages,
edition, language, book size and ISBN number, etc.

4.1b: A subject entry

Classmark
according to
the Dewey
system

Subject

Electronics - ionization   537.532
              of gases

Cherrington B. E.

Gaseous Electronics and Gas Lasers

Book
details

Pergamon; London 1979

Location; Science Library, First Floor

1 copy for loan

As with Author entry additional information such as number of
pages, etc., may be included on the card.

Figure 4.1 Examples of library catalogue entries using the Dewey System.

The subject index gives no information about any particular item, or how extensive the stock might be on a subject. This is discovered by using the subject catalogue.

Subject catalogue

This catalogue brings together details of all the material held by a library on a particular subject. There is one entry for each item, and the items are arranged according to the classification system in use. In a library using the Dewey system the subject catalogue runs numerically starting in the 000s and ending in the 999s. Obviously there will be gaps in numbering for those subjects not represented in the library. Since every item has a separate entry, many will have the same classmark if there are a number of books etc. on the same subject. Figure 4.1(b) shows what a subject entry would look like on a card if classified by the Dewey system.

Uses of the subject index and subject catalogue

* Enables you to discover what a library has on a particular subject. This is a two stage process: first, use the subject index to obtain the relevant classmark; then, secondly, look up the classmark in the subject catalogue to discover what items are in stock.
* From the catalogue you will see whether the stock is textbooks, audio-visual material, special collections, or reference books etc.
* The catalogues will indicate where in the library the material is kept. Always use the subject index and catalogue before going to the shelves.

Additional points about catalogues

* Although some libraries keep their catalogues either on a card system in special filing cabinets, or on microfiche, many are beginning to use computers, with terminals around the library for readers to use. Different computer systems are available and most allow searching by author, subject and sometimes title. Some provide additional information such as if an item is out on loan, or reserved by another reader. Most computer systems are easy to use, with library staff on hand to give assistance.
* Some libraries have additional catalogues e.g. a title catalogue. This can be used to search out a book if only the title is known. If a title catalogue is not available, details can normally be found using a commercial bibliography (e.g. *BBIP*, see p. 33). Although with most scientific books the title gives a good indication as to content, occasionally this is not the case. *The Blind Watchmaker* by R. Dawkins (published by Longmans in 1986) has nothing to do with clocks or vision; it is about natural selection.

With the Dewey system the book is classified at 575.016 2, and at QH 375 using the Library of Congress method.
* Finding periodicals in a library can sometimes be difficult. This is because some libraries shelve them alongside ordinary books, whilst others keep them apart. Current titles are nearly always kept separate from previous bound issues. Ask the librarians if you have any trouble finding what you need. Academic periodicals are very expensive and few libraries have complete runs of every title in their catalogue. The catalogue will, however, detail how many back issues are available and if a particular title is still bought. You will have to use the ILL service for those not in stock.
* Non-book items like audio-visual material will be found either in the main catalogues, or in separate lists. Places like museums, zoos and botanical gardens (described in Chapter 3, p. 42) also classify and catalogue their stock. Their visitors' guides and other handbooks usually list how the various collections are arranged. If you need these sources, ask the staff for assistance.

4.4 SPECIALIZED LIBRARY SERVICES

Most libraries now have photocopying facilities, and some provide a binding service. Libraries may also have on-line, CD-ROM and information services available; ask if you need them.

The inter library loan system (ILL)

All libraries have a limited stock and may not be able to supply all your needs. Fortunately, in the UK most libraries operate the ILL system which allows them to borrow material from other local and national libraries. For example, the British Library Document Supply Centre in West Yorkshire has an immense collection of scientific books, periodicals, theses, reports and other items available for loan. When using the ILL service bear the following points in mind.

The library making the ILL request requires a full bibliographical description of the item you wish to borrow. This should include:

* Author(s) surname(s) and initial(s).
* Date of publication and edition.
* Full title of book, report etc.
* Publisher and place of publication.
* If you need a scientific paper from a periodical, include the full title of the paper and periodical, together with the volume number and inclusive page numbers of the paper.

* The International Standard Book Number (ISBN). Every book has its own unique reference number. The ISBN for the paperback edition of this book is 0–419–14820–5. The ISBN is usually found at the front of a book, near the title and contents pages.

Some libraries provide a special form for you to fill in; ask the staff if you need any help in completing it. The general advice is to provide as much detail as possible. It is also a good idea to keep a record of where you first learnt about the item being ordered; it can sometimes help trace an unusual or difficult request.

The ILL is efficient and requests are dealt with speedily, although occasionally a loan may take several weeks to process. This means you must be organized with your work and order material with time to spare, especially if deadlines have to be met.

The ILL costs money even though many libraries make no charge, or only expect a fee to cover postage. Enquire before you make a request, and make sure the reference cannot be obtained locally.

Your loan may arrive as a book, photocopy or microform. Sometimes you will be expected to use it in the library and not be allowed to take it home.

Most ILL items may be renewed like other library stock. However, popular items may be issued on a 'short loan' and must be returned by a certain date. Be prepared to work quickly with any ILL material.

Science and technology libraries

Most libraries are comprehensive and cover all subjects, in addition to science. The best guide to the libraries in the UK and Ireland is:

Harrold, A. (ed.) 1989. *Libraries in the United Kingdom and the Republic of Ireland*, 15th edition. Library Association, London.

There are, however, a number of libraries which specialize in some aspect of science and technology. They are all over the country and not just near London. A good guide to their location is:

Adkins, R.T. (ed.) 1988. *Guide to Government Departments and other Libraries*. Science Reference and Information Service, British Library, London.

This directory is widely available in public and academic libraries. The contents are well arranged and easy to follow. The 1988 edition has a subject index.

In the UK the best science library is the Science Reference Library which is part of the British Library. It houses one of the largest and most comprehensive collections in the world. It has two reading rooms in London and they are:

Aldwych Reading Room
9 Kean Street
London   WC2B 4AT

and

Holborn Reading Room
25 Southampton Buildings
Chancery Lane
London   WC2A 1AW

The Science Library publishes, free of charge, a great deal of information (including a regular newsletter). If interested, contact:

External Relations and Liaison Service
Science Reference Library
25 Southampton Buildings
Chancery Lane
London   WC2A 1AW

The library also produces, for sale, bibliographies on items of current scientific interest. These are sometimes called 'guidelines', and two recent examples are:

O'Donogue, M. (1988) *Crystal Growth: a guide to the literature.*

Grayson, L. (ed.) 1988. *Acid Rain and the Environment 1984–88. A select bibliography.*

Seminars are also organized, although attendance may be restricted and there is a fee. Recent topics have included 'Chemical Information', and 'The Japanese Science and Technology Industry'.

For people outside London much of the Library's stock is still available on ILL. Most of this comes from the British Library Document Supply Centre (BLDSC) in West Yorkshire. The centre has a reading room open to the public. The address to contact is:

Customer Services
The British Library Document Supply Centre
Boston Spa
Wetherby
West Yorkshire   LS23 7BQ

Copyright libraries

In the UK certain libraries are known as copyright libraries and by law they are entitled to receive a copy of everything published in Great Britain. As a result they have an excellent stock of books and periodicals. Access to these libraries may be restricted so it is best to enquire first. Their addresses are:

The British Library. This is the national library of the UK and includes the Document Supply Centre in West Yorkshire, and the Science Reference Library, London. The central administration address for the library is:

The British Library
2 Sheraton Street
London   W1V 4BH

The Bodleian Library
University of Oxford
Broad Street
Oxford   OX1 3BG

Cambridge University Library
West Road
Cambridge   CB3 9DR

The National Library of Scotland
George IV Bridge
Edinburgh   EH1 1EU

The National Library of Wales
Aberystwyth
Dyfed   SY23 3BU

Trinity College Library
College Street
Dublin 2
(Although in the Republic of Ireland, this library is included in the copyright libraries).

4.5 A USER'S CHECK-LIST

Here is a list of points to remember when using libraries.

* With your main study libraries, have a good look around, making a note of opening times, number of books allowed out on loan and other services such as photocopying and on-line facilities. Ask if they operate a system for reserving books, have short or overnight loans for heavily used and popular items, and subscribe to the ILL service.
* Register to be a reader at the start of your course. Often applications take time to process: don't wait to join until you need to use the library, as this will waste time. If you are issued with a reader's ticket, membership, or identity card have it with you when using the library.
* Abide by library regulations and procedures. Treat stock with respect and be thoughtful of other readers. Simple tasks like replacing a book in its right position helps other students.
* Most libraries provide free guides and leaflets about services and stock. Collect and read them. Some libraries hold induction sessions for new readers; always attend since they will show you how the library operates and give an idea of the range of material in stock.
* Keep an eye on notice boards. Most libraries have on display the latest publisher's brochures, new books and other items. Make a note of anything which could be useful. Be alert to change.
* Get to know the staff and ask for advice if you need it. Be as specific as possible when asking a question. Be polite and thank them for their help.

* When using the catalogues have a pencil and paper handy to jot down classmarks and other details. If not, you will have forgotten them by the time you reach the shelves.
* Never try to remember the different classification systems. With the help of this book, write on a post card the main subject classmarks for the systems used in your libraries. Every time you visit a library have the cards with you – they will save a great deal of time.
* Know where reference books, indexes and all the other information sources (listed in Chapter 3, p. 18) are kept.
* Libraries operate different methods for issuing books and other items. Fill in any issue forms accurately when borrowing material – remember you are responsible for anything taken out in your name. Many libraries now use bar codes and light pens. Return loans on time and collect any receipts, if given, or see that your returns have been properly cancelled.
* With the ILL service, be prepared to wait. Order material in plenty of time when meeting assignment deadlines.
* If you fail to find an item on the shelves then check nearby, it may have been misplaced by the last reader. Ask the staff; it could be out on loan.
* You may decide to visit a library some distance from home. It saves time if you write beforehand, informing them why you need to visit. The library may be able to have some material ready for you on arrival.

SUMMARY

This chapter explains how libraries organize and store scientific information, together with an account of other services they provide.
The key points are:

* know what is meant by classification and cataloguing
* visit all the libraries in your neighbourhood. This includes your college and local public library. They may tell you of other libraries open to students (e.g. local industry, hospital libraries, other colleges)
* practise using their classification and catalogue systems. Become confident in using them, whether on cards, microfiche or computer. Ask the library staff if you have problems. Being able to use the catalogues effectively is the most important library skill to develop
* make and keep a record of the scientific subjects which are well represented, and those which are not
* know how the periodical and non-book materials are catalogued and stored, and the procedures for using them
* discover whether there are special science libraries near you, and any services, special collections, etc., which may prove useful
* getting the best from a library means you must use it, know the stock and other services on offer.

5

Identifying information needs: an action plan

Let us recap on the information story so far. Chapter 3 lists the various information sources, together with their uses, limitations and accessibility. Chapter 4 explains the way libraries store and classify information, and how, by using catalogues and other aids, material may be located. In summary we have described what is available, and how to find it. The most important task, however, is to relate the two. If you are set an assignment, how do you decide what type of information is needed and which are the best sources to get it from? The ability to search out relevant information is one of the most important skills a scientist can have. This chapter describes an action plan to help identify and find the information you need. It may not solve every query, but it will help with most.

The information action plan can be split into a number of stages:

- Stage 1: deciding why you need information
- Stage 2: defining information needs
- Stage 3: choosing which sources to use and searching them out
- Stage 4: collecting the information.

5.1 STAGE 1: DECIDING WHY YOU NEED INFORMATION

An understanding of why information is needed often helps identify the type of material to look for. You use information for assignments and other class work. Although this was briefly mentioned at the beginning of Chapter 3 (see p. 18) let us reconsider this in more detail. Depending on the course, you may have to write essays, carry out and write up practical exercises, give short talks, even complete long-term assignments like projects and dissertations. An examination of the characteristic features of each one may highlight particular information needs. This in turn may help when starting a search, in deciding where to look, and what to look for.

Information may, therefore, be required for:

- an essay
- a dissertation
- practical work (class work and projects)
- talks and similar presentations
- other everyday class work.

The following sections contain suggestions regarding the information demands of each one. In some cases, for instance with the essay and dissertation, there is some overlap and some courses refer to essays, dissertations and projects etc. by alternative names. If you have to complete an assignment not listed here, then don't panic. First read through each section to gain a good idea of what is meant by information needs and then list, for your particular assignment, exactly what sort of information is required. The key to successful retrieval is to adopt a systematic yet flexible approach. Be determined, and never give up easily – persistence pays rewards. With practice, you will develop confidence and competence with your information skills.

An essay

Characteristic features

Essays are not the sole domain of humanities and sociology students; scientists have to write them too! Unlike most other forms of scientific writing, essays are not divided into headed sections; they are pieces of continuous prose. In general, they are discursive rather than descriptive; you have to express ideas and opinions. Essays do not depend solely on the recall of facts, although facts are required to support the views expressed and serve as examples to illustrate salient points in a discussion. If possible use wide-ranging and contrasting examples in support of an argument. When researching material for an essay, do so with a critical and discerning eye.

Information needs

Essays require information which may provide for a topic:

* A general background and introduction.
* Advantages, disadvantages and limitations.
* Commercial and industrial applications.

* Some account of the non-scientific issues involved (e.g. political, social, economic).
* An explanation of the discovery, development and importance of a scientific theory.
* A comparison with another scientific area, and a discussion of any relationships which exist.
* A criticism or debate, especially of contentious scientific issues.

A dissertation

Characteristic features

Some courses require students to complete an independent study which is not based on practical work carried out by themselves. This type of assignment is mostly called a dissertation and can be long (e.g. 4000–8000 words, sometimes longer). Dissertations may investigate any aspect of a scientific topic, such as its history, development and industrial application. Although similar to an essay in the way information is treated, dissertations are longer and usually divided into separate headed sections, including introduction, methodology, results, discussion etc. (see p. 109). Since dissertations are non-practical, relying almost entirely on published material, you must use your information retrieval skills to full effect.

Although a dissertation may seem a daunting task, don't be put off. It can present you with an exciting and interesting academic challenge, allowing you to express original ideas about science. This is especially so if you can choose the title (see p. 92) and research a topic which really interests you. Remember, even though a dissertation relies on published data, it is still an original piece of work in that you have to bring your own interpretation to a topic, drawing on many sources of information which must be rigorously compared and assessed. An interesting feature is that some dissertations may be inter-disciplinary, allowing a discussion of social and political factors, often implicit in an area of science. Examples of dissertation titles could include:

* The use of chemicals in the home.
* The development of the silicon chip.
* The history of the video.
* New forms of energy.
* Industrial uses of enzymes.

(Advice on the writing up of dissertations may help here, and this is described on pages 109–112.)

Information needs (look back at the needs of an essay – many apply here)

Dissertations require:

* A great deal of research data and information from a wide range of primary and secondary sources: the information should be as up-to-date as possible.
* Information which is often inter-disciplinary.
* Extensive background material.
* Material which is discursive and critical.

Practical work

Characteristic features

Practical work can vary. It may be either experiments performed in normal class time, or you may design and carry out longer-term investigations. These longer pieces of work are called projects. Practical work does not always mean being in a laboratory. For example, you may visit different habitats, such as the seashore, to collect data. This is called field work. Alternatively, you may decide to carry out an opinion survey about some aspect of science. Whatever the nature of the practical work, it will always generate new results which need to be evaluated and written up. (See also Chapter 6, p. 102, which gives advice on the writing up of practical work, and Chapter 9, p. 155, for help with projects).

Information needs

Information needs for practical work will also vary. For class work you will probably be given a schedule detailing all the information required. When carrying out a project you will be expected to search out material and, depending on the topic, the following may be needed:

* A general background and up-to-date literature review of the topic: it is important in projects to compare your results with those of other scientists.
* Details of equipment, experimental methods and chemical reagents.
* An account of the experimental design, together with reasons for its choice, and the use of standards, controls and sampling methods.
* Suitable ways of recording, displaying and analysing results.
* Details of relevant mathematical and statistical formulae.
* A knowledge and understanding of the theoretical basis of the investigation.

* Information about current safety procedures and safe working practices – never overlook safety.
* Details of the names of compounds, physical constants and units.
* Information about the geography of an area (for fieldwork), the keeping and preservation of animals and plants (for some biological work), and the construction of sampling frames (for survey work).

Talks and similar presentations

Characteristic features

Many courses now require students to give talks and take part in discussion groups, such as seminars. The ability to do this clearly and concisely is an important communication skill, and like other assignments, requires information. Sometimes a talk may be about a completed project or dissertation, in which case the information will only need re-drafting. (See also Chapter 6, p. 145, which is all about giving talks.)

Information needs

When searching out material for a talk or similar exercise remember:

* The information is meant to be listened to, or seen (if visual aids are used), and not read.
* Find information which is concise and easy to follow, as the time for a talk may be limited (e.g. 15–30 minutes): this means you must be selective in your choice of material.
* If you can use visual aids keep a watch out for information which would convert easily into tables and figures.
* Select interesting and relevant examples which the audience can relate to.
* If other members of the class are expected to join in, decide if you need to research the whole topic or just one part of it.
* Always prepare some background information in case you have to answer questions at the end of the presentation.
* Discover, if possible, what the audience already knows about the topic: this will help in selecting appropriate information.

Class work

Characteristic features

Everyday class work can vary from formal lecture situations to sessions where you are busy working out examples, or doing some other type of exercise. However, you will always need information to supplement the work so, from the start of a course, develop the habit of reading around the subject.

Information needs

Information will be needed for a variety of reasons, and these may include:

* Checking the accuracy of formulae, dates, and labelling on diagrams.
* Searching out additional examples to those given in class.
* Finding out the meanings of new terms.
* Reading relevant background information when beginning a new subject.
* Trying to understand a topic which may have proved difficult to follow the first time through.
* Having to complete extra problems and/or exercises.
* Making your own notes on a topic (Always check in the syllabus to discover exactly what you are expected to know).
* Revising for a test or examination.
* Looking up material in preparation for the next class.

5.2 STAGE 2: DEFINING INFORMATION NEEDS

Knowing the type of information needed, you now have to decide exactly what to search out.

Specific versus general needs

First, ask yourself if the information required is either specific or general. Specific means one-off questions like checking the name of a compound, the value of a constant, or the accuracy of a formula; whereas general means the need to research a wider area, such as magnetism, or the properties of certain compounds. A general need is one where you are uncertain as to exactly what kind of detail is wanted. This situation usually arises when an assignment, like an essay or project, has been set.

Solving specific needs

Specific queries can normally be answered by using either an appropriate textbook or reference book (e.g. encyclopaedia, dictionary, data book). Always know where these sources are kept in your main study library. Most specific enquiries can be dealt with quickly and should not cause any problems.

Solving general needs

General needs involve more thought. If you know the main subject area to be researched, but are uncertain as to which particular aspects need looking up, use the **brainstorming** technique. Correctly used it will identify and solve most general information queries. The technique was introduced to the author several years ago – it rarely fails and was used in the planning of this book. In many ways it is similar to the pattern system of making notes described on p. 14.

How to brainstorm

1. Start with a clean sheet of paper. If you have big handwriting then use A3 (420 × 297 mm) sized paper; you may need the space.
2. Write the title of the assignment in the centre.
3. Read and study the title carefully. Pick out and underline (a coloured pencil makes it stand out) the main subject area (e.g. pH, inorganic metals, electrons).
4. Identify and underline the words which tell you what to do with the subject (e.g. discuss, compare, evaluate).

Note: Already you have begun to define your needs. You know the subject area and what type of knowledge you are looking for. This may seem obvious, but many students when beginning an assignment fail to really understand what they need to do.

Let's take an example: imagine you have to write an essay on 'The advantages of owning a micro-computer'. Faced with this, many students would write down everything they could find out about micro-computers. On re-reading the title only 'The advantages of owning' one must be discussed; anything else is superfluous. So, take care not to panic when beginning an information search. Stop and be sure you understand exactly what is needed; this will make the search more selective and accurate.

5. When confident you know exactly what is required, write down around the title, like the spokes of a wheel, all the facts you already know about the subject, together with any other thoughts and opinions you might have. If useful material has been taught in class, refer back to it and include this on the plan. Write down only main headings and single words. You will use them as 'search terms' later when going through the different information sources. At this stage, apart from class notes, don't use any other sources of information. Try to generate your own ideas. Don't worry if some turn out to be irrelevant; they can always be deleted later. Figure 5.1 shows what the brainstorm plan might look like at this stage for the dissertation topic 'The use of chemicals in the home'.

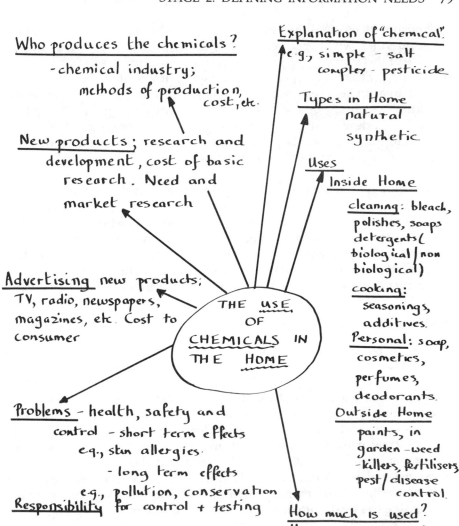

Who produces the chemicals?

- chemical industry;
   methods of production,
                    cost, etc.

New products; research and
   development, cost of basic
   research. Need and
   market research

Advertising new products;
TV, radio, newspapers,
magazines, etc. Cost to
consumer

Explanation of "chemical".
e.g., simple - salt
     complex - pesticide

Types in Home
           natural
        synthetic

Uses
    Inside Home
       cleaning: bleach,
       polishes, soaps
       detergents (
       biological / non
       biological)
       cooking:
          seasonings,
          additives.
       Personal: soap,
          cosmetics,
          perfumes,
          deodorants.
    Outside Home
       paints, in
       garden - weed
       - killers, fertilisers
       pest / disease
               control.

THE USE
OF
CHEMICALS IN
THE HOME

Problems - health, safety and
   control - short term effects
      e.g., skin allergies.
         - long term effects
         e.g., pollution, conservation
Responsibility for control + testing

How much is used?
How much is spent in
the average home?

Figure 5.1 An early brainstorm plan for the dissertation topic 'The Use of Chemicals in the Home'.

6. Next arrange the material in a logical sequence. Do this by dividing and numbering, in order, all the suggestions written down on the plan. Asterisk (*) any areas which have already been covered in class, or researched for previous assignments – delete any areas not needed. Tick (√) areas you intend to keep. If you are not sure, mark them with a

question mark (?). When more information becomes available, you can decide then whether to retain or reject them. Figure 5.2 illustrates the plan at this stage.

7. Starting with number 1 on your plan write down, at the bottom, a list of key areas to be researched (Figure 5.2). This forms a number of 'search terms' which can be used as a starting point when going through the various indexes, subject catalogues, guides, abstracts and other sources of information. Look back and skim through Chapter 3 (see p. 18) to remind yourself of the variety available.

A well thought out brainstorm plan will help in a number of ways:

* It identifies the subject areas which need to be researched.
* It reveals how much information you already have about a topic.
* It provides an overview of the assignment and helps pick out relationships and comparisons: this can be very useful at the writing-up stage.
* It serves as a plan which is also needed at the writing-up stage (see p. 92).

What happens if you become stuck, have no ideas, and can't get started?

Occasionally, all of us seem unable to get started and our minds go a complete blank. What can be done? One suggestion is to use the subject catalogue in the library and search out a book on the area being studied. Be sure to choose one at the right academic level (see p. 40). Quickly skim read the contents and get a general idea of the subject. This may help start the brainstorming. If the library catalogue offers little help, then a bibliography like *BBIP* may come to the rescue with an appropriate title. Sometimes when assignments are set reading lists are given and these can help select an introductory book. An encyclopaedia can also prove a good starting point. If books offer little help, then try other general sources, like a film or video. Discussing the work with other people may also help get you going.

5.3 STAGE 3: CHOOSING WHICH SOURCES TO USE AND SEARCHING THEM OUT

The brainstorming has provided a series of 'keywords' or 'search terms' which need to be searched out. In addition, you know why the information is needed. With these in mind select the best information sources to use. The general advice is to use as many as possible in the time available. Always keep to the latest editions and, if possible, include some primary sources. Searching out information has a snowball effect; one good reference tends to

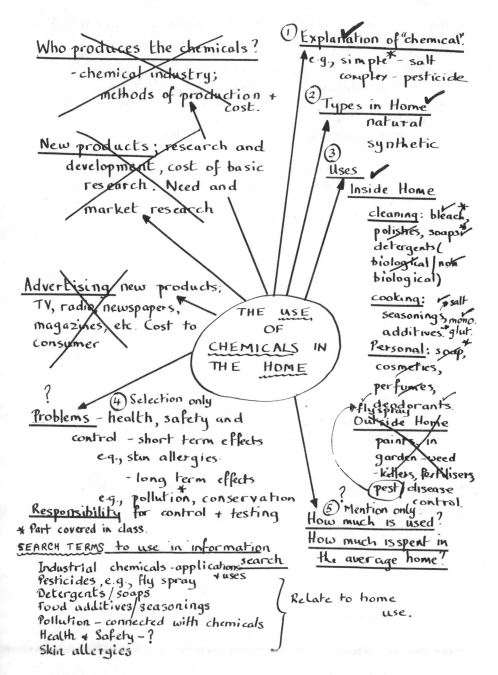

Figure 5.2 A later brainstorm plan (various parts have been deleted, certain parts numbered and search terms identified).

lead to lots of others. Be confident of your library and retrieval skills and check you:

* Know the range of sources available in your main study library – even small ones usually have a lot of information.
* Understand the library's classification system.
* Can use the various catalogues, indexes, abstracts, etc.
* Know how to order material with the ILL service.

Most libraries have at least some of the following: audio-visual material, bibliographies, current awareness publications, guides, indexes, standards, reports, reviews, reference books and textbooks etc. All of these can prove a good starting point when chasing up material.

To help you choose particular information sources the following may help.

If you need **general background/introduction/historical development** *then use:*

Audio-visual material
Museums
Reference books (e.g. encyclopaedia)
Textbooks (at right level).

If you need **to consolidate class work** *then use:*

Learning packages (e.g. audio-visual, computer simulations)
Reference books (all types depending on need)
Textbooks.

If you need **a literature review/account of recent developments** *then use:*

Conference proceedings
Current awareness publications
Periodicals
Reports
Reviews
Theses.

If you need **to construct a reference list/bibliography** *then use:*

Bibliographies (e.g. *BBIP*)
Conference proceedings
Current awareness publications
Official publications
Reports
Reviews.

If you need **recent knowledge/current research/examples/facts and figures**
then use:

Conference proceedings
Current awareness publications
Official publications
Periodicals
Research in progress
Reviews
Statistics
Theses.

If you need **experimental methods/techniques** *then use*:

Audio-visual material
Current awareness publications
Periodicals
Patents
Reference books (e.g. data books)
Standards
Textbooks
Theses
Trade literature.

If you need **industrial/commercial applications** *then use:*

Audio-visual material
Botanical gardens
Museums
Patents
Reports
Reviews
Standards
Science parks
Trade literature.

If you need **non-scientific issues** (e.g. political and social opinion, ethical
problems of science) *then use:*

Newspapers
Official publications
Organizations
People
Reports.

If you need **future possibilities** *then use:*

Research in progress
Trade literature.

If you need **specific data** (e.g. names, addresses, formulae, constants, terminology) *then use:*

Culture collections
Reference books (e.g. data books, directories, dictionaries)
Remote sensing
Videotex
Zoos.

Notes

○ Translations and microfilms have not been included. If you come across or need them, then refer to pages 41 and 49 and ask at your library.
○ On-line searching (see p. 51) can be used for nearly every information need. If it is available and you can use it, then do so. It saves an enormous amount of time.
○ Current awareness publications include abstracts, indexes and current contents (see p. 33).

5.4 STAGE 4: COLLECTING THE INFORMATION

After locating the sources, you are ready to start the process of collecting the information. The points to note are listed below.

○ Make a careful record by writing comprehensive notes, drawing tables and figures. Keep to the same style of note making as used in class (see p. 12); thus when an assignment is complete any new notes can be easily incorporated into existing ones. This will be useful for later work.
○ When making notes always use your own words. Never be tempted to copy out large sections of other people's writing, although this seems attractive when working through a difficult or complicated section. You will never fully understand the science involved, and this will affect later progress which builds upon earlier work. It is permissible, however, to reproduce quotations and data to illustrate a particular point, provided the source of the information is acknowledged. When photocopying be sure you are not breaking the law of copyright; most libraries will supply details about this.
○ If quotations and numbers are involved copy them out accurately.
○ If you have ordered a number of items on ILL, they will arrive at different times, so keep a record of all the requests. Remember, once you get into a search for a long assignment, you may be working through several ILL requests, in addition to material from your own library. Keep calm and work methodically, knowing where each reference fits in with your brainstorming plan.

○ Always relate the information collected to the brainstorm plan. A simple technique is to use numbered or coloured folders – one for each area being searched. The notes for each section are then kept in the separate folders. This method is especially good if one reference contains material over a wide field. Since any notes are eventually filed with your class work, the same folders can be used many times.

○ Condense the information contained in a reference. A description or chronological account can usually be written in table form without losing any content. Tables like this are useful at the writing up stage. (Although the actual writing up comes later, sometimes when working through a reference you develop an idea on how to present and write up certain information. Note down ideas.)

○ Always check through any notes when you have finished with a book etc. Although you should work as quickly as possible, never panic and rush to hand a reference back, only to discover you need it again. By then other students may be using it, or if it is on ILL, it may have been returned to its 'home' library.

○ Always keep a record of every information source used, be it book, periodical, thesis etc. They will be needed to compile the reference list. Details of what to record are given on page 113. It can seem tedious to write down so much detail but never skimp. Remember you are studying science and it is a precise discipline. A well prepared reference list shows to an examiner or reader that you have taken time and effort to gather important and relevant information. This is taken into account, and goes to your credit when the work is assessed. An efficient way of keeping information source details is to use record cards, with one card per reference. The cards can be filed and stored. If you have access to a computer, programmes are available which store this type of information.

○ Always balance time and availability. If there is no time limit (very unlikely) for an assignment you can spend a great deal of time researching many references. Where work has to be handed in by a certain date, always allow time to write it up. In cases like this, limit your search to key items only – good library and retrieval skills will help here.

○ Use every source wisely – study it in terms of suitability, accuracy, relevance and academic level. Pay attention to publication dates and, if possible, include primary and secondary material.

○ Chapter 3 describes a number of non-book sources and how to trace them. Using non-book sources is really no different from using book material. Go through and study them, noting down all the details you need. However, when approaching organizations, industrial companies or individuals, you may need to write a letter in the first instance. In which case:

* Keep the letter simple and polite, explaining that you are a student needing information for a particular assignment.

* Describe briefly what the assignment is about and give a brief account of your course and college.
  If the request is complex then a supporting letter from a teacher is useful.
* Enclose a stamped addressed envelope for a reply.
* If someone does help then write back and say thank you. If they provide a great deal of assistance, then a formal acknowledgement is a good idea (see p. 103).

SUMMARY

This chapter outlines an action plan to work out and identify your information needs.

The key points are:

* the plan is divided into 4 stages:

  * **Stage 1:** deciding why you need information. Why you need information often determines what type to look for.
  * **Stage 2:** defining information needs. Here you decide what you already know, what you need to know, and if your query is either specific or general. Use the brainstorming technique for general needs.
  * **Stage 3:** choosing which sources to use and searching them out. Here you choose to search primary, secondary, book and/or non-book material. Library skills are important here.
  * **Stage 4:** collecting the information. Finally, you work through the selected sources by making notes, etc.

* use this plan the next time you start an assignment
* with practice, searching out information is relatively easy, provided you adopt a systematic approach
* be flexible – one good reference will lead to others
* use a variety of sources – the more advanced your course the more you will be expected to include.

6

Scientific writing

This chapter offers advice in writing up scientific work, as scientists must be able to communicate to each other and also to non-scientists about their work. As with any skill there are a number of things to consider:

- why you need to write
- types of scientific writing
- characteristics of good scientific writing
- how to begin writing
- advice for essays, practical work and dissertations
- quoting references, constructing a bibliography, using quotations etc.

6.1 WHY YOU NEED TO WRITE

Students often query why they need to write assignments, such as essays, in the first place. An appreciation of their importance may make you feel more prepared to put in the work needed.

Scientific writing is important because of the following properties.

○ Helps test those assessment objectives listed in Chapter 1 (see p. 1), especially the ability to communicate clearly and accurately.
○ Provides an opportunity for students to work on their own. It shows if you are capable of independent study; able to search out, evaluate and present information. For example, the way a project is written up gives a good indication as to how well it was designed and carried out.
○ Reveals whether or not you can handle results, express ideas and understand the scientific principles on which your work is based.
○ Requires thorough preparation which in turn will extend your subject knowledge.
○ Is normally marked and the marks may count towards your final grades. It is in your own interest to spend time and effort in writing up your work.

6.2 TYPES OF SCIENTIFIC WRITING

There are different forms of scientific writing and the list below is by no means complete. It does not include the thesis nor scientific paper. It has been limited to those types which most science students have to write. The types include:

* An essay.
* Practical work (both class work and project).
* A dissertation.

You may also have to write a letter (see p. 85), and some courses expect students to prepare brochures and special reports (e.g. a feasibility report). Although the arrangement of material in each type of assignment will vary, there are a number of characteristic features common to all types of formal scientific writing which need to be considered when preparing to write. Some of these apply to examination answers and note-taking. However, since writing notes and answering examination questions are somewhat different, these are dealt with separately in Chapter 2 (p. 12) and Chapter 10 (p. 177).

6.3 CHARACTERISTICS OF GOOD SCIENTIFIC WRITING

Careful planning and thinking through

Time spent in deciding exactly what you want to say will make the writing clearer and easier to understand. It gives the material a sensible and logical order. Thorough planning prevents points being omitted, or placed out of sequence, which may confuse the reader and even yourself. Sound preparation, in the long term, saves time and helps produce a more informed piece of work.

Clarity and conciseness

The reader must be in no doubt as to what you mean. Scientists often deal with complex subjects and it is not always easy to explain and put these into words. For example, an experimental method should be so clearly written that the reader, from the account given, should be able to repeat the same experiment. If this proves difficult, then the writing is ambiguous and needs revision.

Accuracy

If you include measurements then inform the reader about the limits of their accuracy and use the correct units. Data taken from other sources must always be copied out correctly (it is easy to make slips), and the source acknowledged.

Tables and figures

Always explain them thoroughly. Students' work often contains beautifully drawn tables and figures with little or no reference made to them in the writing. It takes a great deal of time to produce neat, well labelled diagrams; be sure to use them. Make full use of your material. Don't, however, include figures and tables simply to expand a piece of work. They must be relevant and an integral part of any assignment. (Chapter 7, p. 119, gives advice on the display of data.)

An appropriate format

Examination Boards normally lay down guidelines for the presentation of written work. These have to be firmly adhered to, since failure to do so may cause a loss of marks. Never give marks away – earn as many as you can. Your teacher will keep you informed of any regulations – be sure you know exactly what is expected from you.

Write in your own words

Never copy out and use other people's writing. Writing styles vary and your work will end up like a patchwork. Also, you will never understand the science involved and this will affect later progress which builds upon earlier work. Examination boards view copying or plagiarism as dishonest work. They regard it as a serious offence and will certainly penalize a guilty student. Students are often confused as to what constitutes plagiarism. Plagiarism is when you copy out, word for word, passages from published work (or work from other students) and pass it off as your own. Although you will use books, papers etc. to provide information about a subject, this is not plagiarism, provided you use your own words when describing and discussing the subject. It is permissible to reproduce quotations and data to illustrate a particular point, provided that the source of reference is always acknowledged. Advice about using quotations is given on page 116.

Presentation

Work, especially if it is to be assessed, should be as neat and tidy as possible. Nearly all mark schemes for written work allocate some marks for general presentation. With care these are relatively easy to gain, and having them could make all the difference between pass and fail. Even if the scientific content of the work is poor, some marks may still be awarded for overall presentation. Points to note about presentation include the following.

○ Leave good margins.
○ Keep to an accepted format (check your examination regulations).
○ Make headings and side headings stand out either by underlining (using a ruler, not freehand) or with capital letters. Word processors, if allowed, offer a good variety of useful printing styles.
○ When writing a long assignment (e.g. a project) decide whether each section should begin on a separate sheet of paper. Number each section, being consistent and using the same system throughout. Students often begin by using Arabic numbers (1, 2, 3, ...) then change to either Roman numerals (I, II, III, ...) or even to letters (A, B, C, ...) half-way through.
○ Ensure that the　pages　are correctly numbered and assembled in the right order before handing in.
○ Make handwriting tidy, keeping to the same colour ink and paper. A change mid-way is off-putting and spoils the general impression. If any corrections are needed then make them neat. Correcting fluid is good if used according to the manufacturer's instructions. If no fluid or good eraser is available then cross the mistake through and re-write it (e.g. sold, solid). Never be tempted to overwrite since this looks messy, and if the occasional word is missed out then use a caret (e.g. the　blue　solution). With a word processor alterations are very straight-forward to make. If you have access to a word processor and are allowed to use it, then do so. Word processors save a lot of time and effort.
○ Be sure that any tables and figures are neatly produced, correctly numbered, labelled and arranged in the right order, and that this corresponds to the written text. (See Chapter 7, page 119 for advice about using tables and figures).

Acknowledging sources of information

Reference is made in the text itself, together with a detailed list at the end of the writing. This list is variously called the bibliography, literature cited, or references. The different styles of quoting and referring to references are explained on page 112. The number of references consulted will depend on the assignment; a class practical may need none, whilst an essay, project or dissertation may require a large number.

The passive voice

This means 'I' is rarely used. Instead of writing 'I measured the amount of water', write 'The amount of water was measured'. This may seem old-fashioned and pedantic. On the contrary, it gives your work an academic style of writing. The use of impersonal nouns and phrases emphasizes the objective and analytical nature of science. This is what science is all about. It is a rational subject based on knowledge, mostly discovered as a result of experimentation.

Meeting deadlines

A difficulty encountered by some students is meeting the date deadlines for set work. Always start an assignment in good time. Final checking, such as paging, and possibly even typing, always takes longer than originally planned. Allow plenty of time to ensure no last-minute panics. Having to meet deadlines may seem harsh on the part of Examination Boards. It is, however, an important part of their total assessment to see how well you can cope and work within a fixed time limit. People employed in industry and commerce often have to produce good quality work within a fixed time schedule.

The author

At the beginning of any writing always give your full name, date and course details. Work for external examinations may need your examination and centre number.

6.4 HOW TO BEGIN WRITING

Writing, like any task, is easier if it can be divided into a number of stages. The processes of scientific writing can be divided into four, namely:

* Stage 1: planning the assignment.
* Stage 2: collecting the information.
* Stage 3: sorting it out.
* Stage 4: the actual writing process.

The amount of time spent at each stage depends on the nature of the assignment. However, whenever you need to write always tackle it in the same way and this will help establish a thorough and effective way of working. Never be tempted to take a fresh sheet of paper, put the title at the top and immediately begin writing the final version. You may start well, but soon the ideas will dry up, the order may need revision, or several other things need changing. With all your work, develop a systematic, planned and logical approach.

A note about titles:

Titles for assignments are normally set by teaching staff, although occasionally you may be able to select one of your own. A word of warning when deciding on a title. Choose it carefully, bearing in mind the information sources available. Always relate your choice to material which is relatively accessible. Don't select a subject only to discover there is little information about it, or what is available is difficult to obtain. Course work usually has to be completed by a set date; don't spend all the time gathering in material, only to have no time left in which to write it up.

A free-choice title should be concise and as self-explanatory as possible. If it has to be submitted before the work is carried out then keep the wording fairly general. Allow room for change, the reason being that when researching out material, certain information may prove difficult to find, or something unexpected which looks particularly interesting and worth including may be uncovered. Too specific a title, which has already been submitted, may limit what can be included in the final work. If the title is handed in when everything is complete, then decide on the exact wording towards the end of writing up. This advice covers all types of written work.

The first two stages have already been worked through in Chapter 5 (p. 12) which describes how to identify and search out information. When studying always relate how the same skill can be used in different situations. Stages 1 and 2 will be briefly revised.

STAGE 1: PLANNING THE ASSIGNMENT

This stage is completed when you brainstorm (see p. 78) to identify the information needs. The final brainstorm plan will also serve as a basis for any written work. To remind you how to brainstorm: first write the title in the centre of a sheet of paper, underlining the key words in the title. Secondly, write around the title all your ideas about the topic. Lastly, arrange the ideas in a logical order, deleting any you think are irrelevant.

Additional points to remember at the planning stage

○ Sort out the work very carefully before beginning to write. With a practical project this means deciding on the design and type of investigation, the collecting together of the apparatus, and working out how the results are to be measured, recorded and possibly interpreted. (Chapter 9, p. 155, gives specific advice on projects.)

○ Be certain what type of finished work you are expected to produce. If possible, study the work of previously successful students to obtain an impression of what completed assignments should look like. If the assignment is something like a project which is written up in a fixed order, namely, introduction, methods, results etc. then use these headings at the planning stage to provide an outline on which to base the work.

○ Study any title thoroughly and determine exactly what you have to do. Are you describing a series of facts, presenting an argument, analysing a set of results, or discussing various opinions? A clear idea of what you are trying to achieve will help produce an end result which is more direct, convincing and original.

○ Make sure how a piece of writing fits in with the course as a whole. If, for instance, an assignment is set on a section of the syllabus not being taught in class, then read the syllabus to discover exactly what is required.

○ It is also good practice at this stage to discuss your plan with a teacher who may make useful suggestions and ensure the work is on the right lines. If, because of examination regulations, they are not allowed to help, they will soon tell you.

Successful planning assists by identifying the main theme of the writing and helps work out exactly what it will contain. A good plan indicates how the work can be divided into sections. The importance and relationship of each part becomes clearer, and this helps in writing the discussion and conclusion. If the assignment is a practical investigation, the plan will contain details such as equipment, resources and methods. As explained in Chapter 5 (see p. 80) a well thought-out brainstorm plan also determines your information needs. It reveals how much information is already present in class or other notes and pin-points gaps in your knowledge, identifying those areas which need to be researched.

Figures 5.1, 5.2 and 6.4 are plans prepared for specimen dissertations to give some idea what they may look like at this stage.

STAGE 2: COLLECTING THE INFORMATION

Using your retrieval skills you can now collect the necessary information (Chapter 5, p. 84). Work methodically, keeping a record of every information source used. Bear in mind the type of information required and how it fits in with the assignment as a whole.

If you are carrying out a project, this is the stage when data are recorded. For example, make full notes as you perform any experiment, ensuring that no important point is omitted. Writing up an experiment from memory is a risky business! Full details of the apparatus used, together with a well labelled diagram or photograph of any special equipment, should be recorded. Keep a note of all suppliers, chemicals and reagents, together with the amounts and concentrations used. When recording results, do so accurately. For example, with a biological investigation using living animals or plants, note how they have been kept before, and during, the experiment. Record temperature, feeding regime, age and sex. All these are important points, which may influence the outcome of the investigation.

A final note about the planning and collecting stages:

Although these two stages have been described separately, they are very much inter-linked. For example, you may need to search out details about a standard experimental method before devising your own investigation. Keep a flexible approach at the planning and collecting stages; a good scheme of work always allows for the incorporation of additional information.

STAGE 3: SORTING IT OUT

The next stage is to sort out and arrange the material in a suitable order for writing up. A suggested scheme is as follows.

○ Re-read all the material, whilst keeping a mindful eye on the brainstorm plan. Be sure you understand all the information and how it relates to the title of the work. You may decide that the same information can be used throughout, in different sections of the assignment. This is fine – the same reference acknowledged several times gives scientific writing coherence.
○ Make new notes to summarize any of the information, if this helps you to identify salient points and ensures your understanding of the work. It may be necessary at this stage to search out new material if some parts seem short of detail.
○ Work carefully through any numerical data, making any necessary calculations. Double-check to prevent any arithmetical errors.
○ If there is a great deal of raw data try to summarize it by drawing tables and/or figures. At this stage only quick sketches are required. Computer programmes are available which can do this for you. When you have finally decided which displays the work to its best advantage, only then make final neat copies. When sifting through data, never throw any away as being useless. Keep everything until the assignment is finally written up. Although much of the data will be presented and summarized in table and figure form, all of it should be retained and, in projects and dissertations, may be needed as an appendix.

1. Title page.
2. Acknowledgements:- industries, supervisor, local library.
   (Mr. J. Smith - special collection)
3. Contents.
4. Abstract.
5. Introduction:- range of use, current cost/use per home, product variety and range. Draw tables, pie/bar charts of % use. Inside use only.
6. Methods:- sources used, e.g. local library special industrial collection, HMSO statistics, Industries contacted + replies received.
7. Types and Uses:- (Link together rather than have separate sections)

   List types - 1 example of each - give name, formula + brief mention of manufacture. Restrict to inside home use only - refer back to introduction sources.

   link with 'trade' examples.

   eg's - bleach,
   soap,
   non-biological detergent,
   salt,
   monosodium glutamate,
   deodorant,
   fly spray (inside use only).

8. Problems: - brief description of all problems - but only 2 given in detail - soap + skin rashes, include more if information becomes available   fly spray + pollution (food chains, etc.)
9. Conclusions:- Wide Use:- expanding chemical industry. Need for control. Responsibility of ?- individual, industry, government. keep brief
10. References - see record cards
11. Appendix - Letter to industries + replies.

Figure 6.1 A possible linear plan for the dissertation topic 'The Use of Chemicals in the Home'.

○ Whilst going through the information try to interpret what it all means. Decide on any apparent trends, conclusions and recommendations. For example, if you have carried out an experiment investigating chemical activity against time, note how it changed over time. Did it increase, decrease, or remain the same? Never forget to record the obvious.

○ Finally, convert all the collected information into a linear plan (Figures 6.1, 6.2). A **linear plan** is a series of points in the order they appear in the final write-up. Depending on the complexity of the assignment the plan may be either a list of key words or a number of headings, each with a summary. The plans should include all examples, although there is little point in re-copying out details just for the sake of it. An asterisk (*) in the plan to remind you when to include a particular example will suffice. Also note in the plan where tables and figures will appear. Certain students may consider linear plans a time-wasting exercise. On the contrary they consolidate and organize your thoughts, and provide a good indication of what the final work will look like. The plans are also useful if you need to prepare a contents page.

STAGE 4: THE ACTUAL WRITING PROCESS

When sorting out is complete, the process of writing can begin.

First, following the linear plan, a draft copy is prepared and this is checked over (sometimes by a teacher). Then, bearing in mind any criticisms, a final version is produced which is either handwritten, typed, or better still word-processed, and handed in for marking. If possible, use a word processor; alterations can be made without the chore of having to re-copy out long passages. This book was written using a micro-computer fitted with a word-processing programme.

The writing up of everyday class practicals may not require drafts, and the final account can be produced at the first attempt. It is still necessary, however, to plan the work, and collect and interpret the results. It is also a good idea to make a linear plan, noting all the main points to be included. With other work, depending on the assignment, it may be necessary to write several drafts. Providing you are within any date deadlines, don't worry if a number are needed. If time becomes short then make the last draft the final version. Even if you think it poor, it will earn some marks – a missing piece of work scores zero!

When preparing drafts always include references, tables, figures and quotations. This gives a clearer impression of what the final work will look like. Write on one side of the paper only, using every other line – this allows plenty of space for alterations and changes. When revising a draft, re-work a section at a time amending spelling, content and presentation. Whether

1. Title page
2. Acknowledgements :- supervisor.
3. Contents.
4. Abstract.
5. Introduction : - explanation of energy. } theoretical
   - different types of energy } basis
   - current uses + demands
   - potential uses with special reference to
     nuclear power compared with gas, coal, etc
6. Methods :- - Use of government sources, contact
   nuclear power industry. Use of
   newspaper, indexes, EEC publications, etc.

7. A Case Study :- The case for Nuclear Energy
   { History. - (table needed of dates +
   { Development science involved discoveries)
   - Current Use :- need map of power
     stations in UK.

   Use newspapers

   - Problems :- disasters = public
     opinion /awareness. Solutions - need
     for research.

   radiation
   - need science)
   involved

   - advantages /limitations- relate to
     basic science.

8. A Comparison of nuclear and other forms of energy.
   - Relate to scientific principles + then
     uses and applications.
9. Future possibilities :- Current research re. nuclear power.
   if available
10. Conclusions :- Advantages (scientific and non-scientific)
    of nuclear power. A summary of case
    study.

11 References.

Figure 6.2 A possible linear plan for the dissertation topic 'New Forms of Energy'.

preparing a draft or final version there are a number of points to consider:

○ Keep the language simple and as clear as possible. Remember you are writing about science, and science should be accurate and precise.
○ Make your sentences reasonably short. Avoid long, rambling sentences and try not to use jargon or clichés.
○ Always use paragraphs. A general guide is to keep to one idea per paragraph.
○ Keep the punctuation simple.
○ Try to spell correctly, especially scientific words. A useful technique is to compile, during your course, a list of words you always find difficult. Keep this handy when writing; it can be quicker than using a dictionary. A good dictionary is, however, essential for a new or difficult word.
○ If you have difficulty finding the right word then a thesaurus, properly used, provides a good list of alternatives. Failing this, put in a word that is nearly correct and either asterisk or underline it. When revising the draft you will notice the word, and by then possibly think of the right one. (With word processors, software is available which checks spelling, and/or acts as a thesaurus.)
○ You may find some sections seem more straightforward to write than others. For example, methods or results are usually easier than the conclusion and discussion. If this is the case then complete the easier sections first. Some parts, like the introduction, can be particularly difficult, so leave these until the end. When the work is nearly complete is often the best time to begin the introduction. By then you will know what the work contains, and, therefore, be better equipped to write the beginning. It is certainly best to compile the contents, acknowledgements, summary/abstract and number the pages when the work is nearly finished.
○ It is sometimes awkward to link one section, paragraph, or sentence with another. Put either a cross or asterisk in the margin of the text to identify the part. When revising the draft, difficulties like this often resolve themselves and you normally come up with the right word(s). It is better, in the first place, to write up the whole thing which needs improvement, rather than spend a long time perfecting a single sentence.
○ A problem you may face is keeping within a fixed number of pages, or words. Normally some leeway is allowed and examination regulations advise on this. What can be done, however, if you have overrun, or are under the fixed target by a large amount? If the draft is too long then go through deleting words like 'very' and adverbs like 'probably'. These can sometimes be removed without the writing losing any sense or meaning. Also summarize the examples more concisely. For instance, a sequence of events like the history of a scientific discovery can be presented in table form, as opposed to a long description. If the draft is too short, then re-

read it carefully, making sure it contains enough information. Check that the examples are sufficiently detailed and the work has not been rushed or skimped. As you write, keep a word count for each section; this may help you to keep within fixed limits. (Some word processors count the number of words for you.) Finally, never make your writing lengthy just for the sake of it. If the account is sound, the case convincing and it is supported with relevant examples, this is the important thing.

o When using abbreviations or acronyms give the words or title in full, e.g. World Health Organization (WHO), at the first mention, using only the abbreviation or acronym thereafter. If a larger number are used then, in addition, provide a glossary listing all of them in alphabetical order. This is normally found at the end, as an appendix. Biologists should pay particular attention when using the scientific name of an organism. Never assume the reader knows what *E. coli* means. Always give the full name (in this case *Escherichia coli*) the first time it appears in the text. Also remember that the generic name always begins with a capital letter even in the middle of a sentence, and the species name with a small letter. *Escherichia coli* may be shortened to *E. coli* any subsequent time it is used. If two organisms are being written about, and the generic name of each begins with the same letter (e.g. *Acrochaetium* and *Audouinella*) be careful not to confuse your reader with the abbreviations. In cases like this always give the generic names in full. It is also customary to underline, or print in italics, the scientific name of an organism. Non-scientific or trivial names (e.g. dandelion, daisy) may be used, unless this causes confusion. For example, the bluebell of England and the bluebell of Scotland are two different plants; in cases like this keep to the scientific names. Trivial names only have a capital letter if they start a sentence.

o Students are often uncertain about using the trade or proprietary names of products. For example, write 'Catchit' at the first mention and from then on use catchit. Other points of style (e.g. the use of quotations, references, footnotes etc.) are described towards the end of this chapter on page 112.

o It is an excellent idea to ask a friend or relative (preferably a non-scientist) to give a final read through of any written work. Working on the same piece of writing for a long time can make you become 'word blind' and miss obvious errors like simple misspellings and the occasional word missed out. A fresh eye looking over the writing will help pick out these slips. Also, a non-scientist will be able to judge whether the writing is well expressed and clear to follow.

Most written work will be marked and returned. Read any comments carefully; they are meant to be constructive and helpful. If the mark is low and the remarks critical, although you may be disappointed, don't get annoyed, but take a positive approach. Ask your teacher why the mark was poor and what must be done to improve the work. It is important when studying that you learn from any mistakes so as not to repeat them. Similarly, if the mark was high ask why the work was particularly good. Use marks as a feedback to help monitor your progress and effort.

6.5 ADVICE FOR ESSAYS, PRACTICAL WORK AND DISSERTATIONS

> Note: It may be useful to study this section in conjunction with Chapter 5, page 72, which explains the information needs of each type of scientific writing.

Whether writing an essay, practical work or a dissertation the characteristic features of scientific writing still apply and the method of preparation (planning, collecting information, sorting out and writing) is the same.

The essay

With essays you need to accomplish two things. First, you have to assemble and organize scientific information. Secondly, you use this information to explore a certain line of discussion. An essay is not usually a straightforward factual account, rather a piece of writing which uses facts to support and illustrate a particular viewpoint.
   When writing an essay, always bear the following in mind.

o Pay particular attention to the title. Thoroughly understand it and decide what has to be done.
o Plan very carefully, developing your own ideas rather than depending entirely on other sources. Look for relationships and links between topics.
o Search out good and contrasting examples. In marking essays examiners particularly note how students use examples to back up their ideas.
o Make the linear plan very detailed, deciding what material should go into each paragraph. This helps when you begin writing.

The essay format

Although an essay is not separated into headed sections it still has a form of its own. It is normally arranged into 3 parts:

1. The introduction, which describes the approach to, and provides an outline of the work.

2. The middle section, which is the largest part of the essay, and deals with the main discussion.
3. The conclusion, where any important points and recommendations are briefly summarized.

Introduction

The opening paragraph(s) form(s) the introduction. A good introduction will explain precisely to the reader what the essay is about, the general theme it will take, and the various issues to be covered. It should provide the reader with a series of 'pigeon holes' in which to put the various ideas expressed. If the essay title is so general that you decide to be selective in the choice of material, then inform the reader at the start, giving your reasons. Don't let them discover for themselves that the treatment has been limited. They may be confused and find the writing difficult to follow, or worse, conclude that important material has been omitted. Always inform the reader of your intentions.

Middle section

This section forms the main part of the essay. Although the work is not sectioned, make great use of paragraphs as a technique to divide up the writing. A good practice is to develop one idea, or concept, per paragraph. Small paragraphs (they can be as short as one sentence) can be used to introduce various topics, for example 'Enzyme activity may depend on pH, temperature and the presence of heavy metals'. If this was a genuine essay, separate paragraphs could then be written about pH, temperature and heavy metals.

Make sure that all the examples are used to their best advantage. Many students just quote them without really explaining how they fit in with the general theme, for instance 'heavy metals, e.g., lead, inhibit enzyme activity'. A good student would continue and explain exactly how lead inhibits activity. Always discuss thoroughly any examples. This is what writing an essay is all about. Figures and tables can be included, provided they are relevant and help emphasize an important point in a discussion. Also use quotations in support of the work; science students don't use them nearly enough in their writing. Page 116 gives advice about using quotations.

Conclusion

Students often find the conclusion difficult to write. They feel they need to write something very impressive and important, like some new exciting scientific discovery. This is not the case. A good conclusion is often no more than a concise summary, highlighting the important points raised. The final paragraph(s) should be used to remind the reader of the topics which have been discussed. If the essay has been a debate, arguing for and against a particular issue, then the conclusion should be used to come down either on one side or the other. Never worry about making a controversial statement in the conclusion. If the essay is a well reasoned account, backed up by suitable examples, and the views expressed are properly informed, it is this the reader wants to see. Lastly, at the end of an essay include a reference list (see p. 113).

Practical work

You will most likely have to write up two types of practical work: short exercises carried out in normal class time, and longer independent investigations often known as projects. Both types, when written up, are always divided into headed sections.

A class practical is normally divided into:

* Aim or Title.
* Introduction.
* Materials and methods.
* Results.
* Conclusions.
* Discussion.

A project, being longer, has more sections (sometimes called chapters):

* Title.
* Acknowledgements.
* Contents.
* Summary or abstract.
* Objectives.
* Introduction, background or scope of study.
* Methods, materials and methods, or method of data collection.
* Results.
* Conclusions.
* Discussion.
* References, literature cited or bibliography.
* Lists of tables and figures.
* Appendices.

You will notice, both for the class practical and project, a number of section headings are similar, or even the same, and some sections can have alternative titles (e.g. Introduction, Background, Scope of study). Your teacher will advise which is the best for you, and Examination Boards often provide recommendations. Also, some scientists would change the order slightly (e.g. put acknowledgements towards the end). These are minor points and the following advice should still prove useful when writing up practical work. Go through selecting what you need.

Aim or Title

Class practicals are usually given an aim, for example, 'An experiment to investigate the properties of a magnet'. A project is given a title, for example, 'Experimental studies on certain halogen gases'. (If you are allowed to choose the title then bear in mind the advice on page 92.)

Acknowledgements

It is customary and good manners to thank everyone who helped in the preparation of your work. If someone outside your college provided a great deal of assistance then give them the opportunity to read the final version. No-one likes being taken for granted, so include everyone who deserves a mention. The acknowledgement might read:

'The author would like to thank Mr A. Green for help with the experimental design and Dr S. Orange MA for general advice during the preparation of this assignment'.

Check that you have spelt the names correctly and have used the right initials, title and qualifications. Acknowledgements are normally only included in longer assignments, like projects (and dissertations).

Contents

All projects have a contents page, which lists the various sections of the work, together with page numbers. Sections, and sometimes sub-sections, are numbered consecutively using Arabic numbers. Appendices are normally referred to by Roman numerals. The contents page is one of the first the reader sees, so create a good impression; layout and neat presentation are important. Experiment with different arrangements until you are satisfied the final choice is best for a particular piece of work. Look at the contents page of this and other books to gain an impression of what they should be like. The contents page should be accurate, so double-check that all sections are present, in the right order, and with the correct pagination. It is easy to get them misplaced and paginated wrongly. Errors like this mar the overall effect. They give the impression that the work has been rushed and carelessly put together. The best time to compile the contents page is towards the end when the final draft is written. Enlist the help of a friend or relative; this will prevent small mistakes being made. The linear plan made earlier (see p. 96) helps in working out the contents page.

Summary or abstract

Projects always contain an abstract or summary, and this is normally found near the beginning. It should be about 5% of the final word count in length, and provides a *précis* of the work. An abstract should be complete in its own right, describing the main theme, and summarizing the results and conclusions. Don't include any tables or figures. The abstract is one of the last sections you should write.

Objectives

Projects occasionally contain an objective section which identifies the scope and purpose of the work. Objectives describe precisely the intention and terms of reference of a study. In most projects objectives are incorporated into the introduction. If a separate section is required then always check, when the work is finished, that the stated objectives agree with the final draft. If not, then re-word and modify them accordingly. Figure 6.3, taken from a biochemistry project, shows the setting out of an objectives section.

Introduction, background or scope of study

As with an essay the purpose of the introduction is to outline what the work is about. It is best to write this section when the methodology, results and conclusions are complete. By then you will have a clearer idea of how all the work relates together. Although this section can be difficult to write, there are a number of points it should cover.

○ It should contain a literature review, describing related and similar published work. (Use library skills to good advantage here.) A thorough discussion of selected studies will demonstrate that you have a good grasp of the subject area and help explain the value of your work.

```
OBJECTIVES

The broad objective of the study is to investigate the enzyme
alkaline phosphatase. More specifically the study sets out to
identify for the enzyme:

     (i)    The kinetic and other characteristics.

     (ii)   The methods which can be used to purify it.

     (iii)  The co-factor requirements.

     (iv)   The current medical applications.
```

Figure 6.3 Setting out the objectives section. An example taken from a project entitled 'A Study on the Enzyme alkaline phosphatase'.

○ It must outline the experimental design and approach being taken, together with reasons for the choice of a particular method. The advantages and limitations of any technique must be explained, especially if specialized equipment is being used.
○ Any technical terminology should be defined and reference must be made to any theoretical assumptions present in the work.
○ If field work is involved then an account of the geography of the area and the location of the habitat is required.

Although always needed with a project, an introduction is sometimes included with class practicals, especially if a series of experiments on one topic are being carried out. The introduction can be quite short, mainly describing associated theory work.

Methods, Materials and methods, or Method of data collection

This part is relatively easy to write, and a good place to begin. A well-written method is so clear and logically organized, that the reader, from the account given, should be able to carry out the same procedures and techniques. The methodology section explains simply what you did and the order in which you did it. Depending on the investigation it should include the following.

○ A full description of the apparatus used, together with a labelled diagram or photograph of any special equipment. Students often write 'The apparatus was used as shown in the diagram'. This is fine, provided the diagram is well drawn and fully labelled. However, a diagram does not always explain how the equipment was set up, how it works and the correct way to use it. Ensure you include enough detail.
○ Experimental conditions such as temperature and pH, together with details of chemicals and reagents, all need describing. Although the names and concentrations of any chemicals and reagents must be given, the recipes for making them up, and details of any special suppliers, can appear in an appendix. If the experiments involve living plants and animals, full information about their condition (e.g. age, sex, fresh or preserved, method of preparation) is also needed.
○ If the practical involves measuring and recording, then details regarding sampling techniques, sample sizes, method of recording data and number of measurements taken must be included. Details of special quantitative techniques, mathematical formulae, statistical procedures and computer programmes also need listing.
○ It is extremely important that all safety precautions and procedures are thoroughly described. Never fail to include safety when writing up a practical – many students do.

Results

Results are either **quantitative** (i.e. they can be measured) or **qualitative** (i.e. the changes you see).

Often an experiment will involve both types of results. For instance, in a biology practical, cells may be counted and sized (quantitative) and their changes in shape and structure (qualitative) described. In a chemical investigation colour changes may be noted (qualitative) whilst recording the time taken for the changes to occur (quantitative). A full record of the results must be kept as the work proceeds or important details will be omitted, and the end result poor. In class practicals it is often possible to write the findings into either your file or notebook as you go along. In projects, it is better to make a draft copy and produce a final version at a later stage. Projects tend to produce a mass of data which usually needs summarizing in some way. Often, results need to be presented as tables and figures, so also study p. 119.

Quantitative results

These include numbers in some form. The particular points to note are as listed below.

○ If there are values smaller than one, insert a 0 (e.g. 0.25 not .25).
○ Values with many zeros can be abbreviated (e.g. 49100000 is better written 4.91×10^7, and 0.25×10^{-5} is preferable to 0.000025).
○ Ensure you are working to an acceptable level of accuracy. For instance, 8, 8.0, 8.00, all indicate different degrees of accuracy. Be clear in your mind the difference between significant figures and decimal places. Accuracy is very important in science. Be as precise as you can.
○ Carefully distinguish between zero and negative results. Zero results should be shown as 0 and negative as $(-)$. Similarly does $(+)$ mean present or positive? Always give a key to explain any symbols used. When using chemical symbols check whether to use a capital or lower case letter. Many students write Co_2 not realizing it should be written CO_2. Certain mathematical symbols can be tricky, so always check you are correct. Pay attention to subscripts (e.g. H_2O) and superscripts (e.g. Ca^{2+}).
○ Always include units, where appropriate, since numbers alone mean almost nothing. Sometimes, where the result is a ratio, there will be no units. Certain units may require explanation. For instance, % on its own is too vague. It could mean either % by volume or % by weight, etc. When using the word 'percentage' and its symbol (%), it is good practice to use the symbol when preceded by a number (e.g. 13 % by volume) and the word when no number is given (e.g. 'The percentage of respondents in the survey ...'). Finally, where possible, use the SI (Système

Internationale d'Unités) system of units. In most branches of science this has replaced older methods and is now internationally accepted. Appendix I, page 181, offers help with units.

○ A project generates a lot of data which has to be sorted out. Although raw data are not normally included in the results section, they should be available to the reader in an appendix.

○ When using mathematical formulae and making calculations, double check that they are correct, and that no arithmetical slips have been made. Even with the use of calculators it is very easy to press the wrong key!

○ Only spell out numbers if it helps to avoid confusion. For example, 'After 5 days, 4 samples out of 10 had changed; 3 out of 10 had not, and 3 out of 10 were starting to change' would be better written 'After five days, four samples out of 10 had changed; three out of 10 had not, and three out of 10 were starting to change'.

Qualitative results

Scientists note and record visible changes, for example, differences in colour and appearance. These can be difficult to describe accurately. For instance, although most people appreciate what is meant by red, orange, green and blue, certain colours described as red-orange, orange-red, blue-green or green-blue tend to mean different things to different people. Be as precise and as simple as possible when making observations. If practicable, record any changes, such as shape and appearance, by well labelled drawings and sketches. Now that Polaroid® cameras are in common use, photographs are also a good idea. The main points to note at the writing-up stage are:

* Keep all drawings and sketches large, neat and accurate.
* Give a full heading.
* Unless you are a very good artist keep shading to a minimum – it can look like scribble!
* Always fully label any drawings, being careful to keep labelling lines straight (use a ruler), and avoid having them crossing over each other.

Conclusions

A mistake made by many students when completing this section is simply to re-write the results. A good conclusion does not repeat the findings, but describes what they show and what can be derived from them. It is good practice, however, to refer to a specific result in order to support a particular point or idea. With a class practical conclusions might only be tentative, but they still need to be written in a professional way. When writing this section, bear the following in mind.

o Only refer to your own results. You compare them with those of other scientists in the discussion section.
o Show how the results relate to the initial objectives and ideas of the study. Do they agree or disagree, and how do the findings indicate this? Comment on any statistical tests carried out.
o Explain your results in terms of their reliability and sources of error. Are there any discrepancies or irregularities which are difficult to account for? Unusual results can often alert you to a significant finding and help suggest further lines of study.
o Never ignore negative results. It is equally important to know that a particular chemical sample does not contain nitrogen, as to know that it does.
o Attempt to provide a theoretical explanation (not always easy) of your results.

Discussion

In this section you explain your results in a wider context.

o Compare your work with that of other scientists. Relate how the results from your investigation agree or disagree with the published findings. If they are different, can you offer any explanations or theories to account for the variation?
o Try to provide suggestions for future research which could be carried out as a result of your work.
o If possible, discuss how your work may be important for industrial application.

A final note about the conclusion and discussion sections:
Many students think that these sections should be long and wordy. This is not so. Although you should not skimp, always be as concise as possible and, with some class practicals, it is possible that a separate discussion is not always needed. With assessed work a good proportion of the marks is normally awarded for these sections, so write them as well as you can.

References, literature cited or bibliography

All formal scientific writing, with the exception of examination answers and most class practicals, should acknowledge and include details of the information sources used. How to do this is described on p. 113.

Lists of tables and figures

Some Examination Boards require candidates to list separately the tables and figures included in a piece of work. Figures include diagrams, graphs, maps and all other illustrations. List the tables first, followed by the figures. The number, title and page reference for each table and figure should be given. Also, the word 'Figure' is sometimes abbreviated to 'Fig.'. The following style is usually accepted.

Tables

Table 1: A comparison of the properties of metallic and non-metallic elements . . . page 3.
Table 2: Seasonal variation of abundance of 19 species of small mammals . . . . page 45.

Figures

Figure 1: Diagram of the apparatus used to measure the conductivity of an electrolyte . page 6.
Figure 2: Graph to show the solubility curve of sodium chloride . . . . page 13.

Appendices

Appendices are important in that they can be used for supplementary information which would be out of place and cumbersome in the main text. Appendices are given a full heading and numbered with Roman numerals (I, II, III etc.). They are included in the contents page and in the pagination. The type of material found in appendices may be:

* Raw experimental data (in table form with each table being properly headed and set out).
* A glossary of technical terms (arranged alphabetically).
* A list of abbreviations and/or acronyms (arranged alphabetically).
* Details of suppliers of equipment and special materials (arranged alphabetically).
* Recipes for unusual reagents and chemicals (arranged alphabetically).
* An updating report – occasionally, when a piece of work is finished and written up, additional material comes to light that is worthy of mention which can be included in an appendix.

The dissertation

The method of producing a dissertation is the same as with the other written work, namely planning, collecting the material, sorting it out and the actual writing process.

Dissertation format

Like a project a dissertation is divided into headed sections (or chapters). It is difficult to give a definitive format for a dissertation, since the way the material is organized depends on the nature of the topic being investigated. In many instances, however, dissertations will have a similar arrangement as a project, namely:

* Title.
* Acknowledgements.
* Contents.
* Summary or Abstract.
* Objectives.
* Introduction.
* Methods.
* Results.
* Conclusions.
* Discussion.
* References.
* List of tables and figures.
* Appendices.

Much of the advice given in this chapter still applies. Even though a dissertation is non-experimental, a methods section is still needed outlining the approach being taken, showing how the various sources of information and data were located. Although it may be shorter than found in a project, it must still be precise and unambiguous.

To give a better idea of the possible arrangement of material in a dissertation, examples of possible titles are given. Brainstorm plans for each have been produced suggesting the various ideas which could be researched. Linear plans, for the writing up stage, are also included. In every case the final dissertation would depend on the availability of information.

It is essential with a dissertation, which depends largely on published information sources, that content reflects what is readily available. Never be tempted to stray into areas where information will be difficult to find. The depth and coverage of a dissertation will also depend on the level of your course. Work for a degree will be more comprehensive, and demonstrate greater analytical and interpretative skills than for GCSE. Look through the work of previously successful students to become familiar with the standard you are expected to produce.

With the following examples, suggestions are given of further work which could be carried out. It would also be possible, by including well thought-out surveys, to convert each dissertation into a project. The surveys could collect local information and opinion about each topic. In such cases the methods section would need to contain a detailed account of the sampling techniques used.

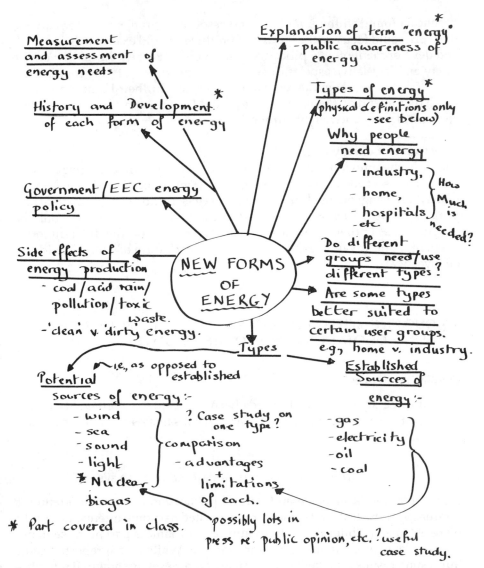

Figure 6.4 An early brainstorm plan for the dissertation topic 'New Forms of Energy'.

The use of chemicals in the home

The brainstorm plans (see Figures 5.1, 5.2) show the various ideas and possible content which could be included. Depending on the amount of time available, and the number of words allowed, some selection of material would be necessary. The linear plan (Figure 6.1) concentrates on the type of chemicals found in the home and the associated problems. Alternatively, the work could focus on the industrial production, and examine the research and development of new products. There could also be a discussion on the safety and legislative aspects. If surveys were carried out they could determine the type of chemicals people buy and use in their homes, and how much they spend on them. The surveys could range from questioning fellow students, family and neighbourhood.

New forms of energy

As with the previous example, the early brainstorm plan (Figure 6.4) contains lots of ideas and the linear plan (Figure 6.2) is only a selection, mainly focusing on nuclear energy. Surveys could also be carried out. Various groups, such as those listed in the first example above, could be questioned as to their awareness of, and preference for, the different forms of energy. The advantages and limitations of each form of energy could also be investigated.

6.6 QUOTING REFERENCES, CONSTRUCTING A BIBLIOGRAPHY, USING QUOTATIONS AND POINTS OF STYLE

Quoting references

One of three styles is usually used. Each is acceptable, provided you are consistent (keep to one throughout), and that it satisfies any relevant course regulations.

The Harvard or author's surname and date of publication system

Here the author's surname and date of publication are used to identify a reference. In the text a reference would be cited as 'Some interesting results were obtained (White, 1985)'. If the author's surname is part of the sentence then the date alone is sufficient, for example 'White (1985) reported some interesting results'. It is customary to use parentheses as shown. If reference to a specific page or diagram is required, as opposed to the whole work, then the following technique applies; 'analysis of the results (White, 1985, p. 13, table 2)', or 'White (1985, p. 13, table 2) in his results indicated …'.

At the end of the text the information sources are listed alphabetically by surnames. If the same author has published several works in one year they are identified as 1952a, 1952b, 1952c and so on, both in the written text and in the list at the end of the writing. An advantage with this method is that references can be easily added or removed. The bibliography of this book is set out using the Harvard system.

The number superscript or Vancouver system

This method arranges the information sources numerically. Each reference is given a number, and always referred to by that number. Number 1 is the first source mentioned, number 2 the second, and so on. In the text the reference would be acknowledged either as; 'some interesting results were obtained [1] [1] , or 'White [1] [1] reported some interesting results'. The numbers are always enclosed in either square brackets or parentheses. Either is acceptable provided you are consistent, and it agrees with any examination regulations. The numbers may be positioned slightly above the writing, and this is why the method is sometimes called the superscript system.

If the same reference is mentioned more than once in a piece of work it is always given its original number. At the end of the text the numbers are listed in ascending order (1, 2, 3 and so on) and full details of each reference are given. A disadvantage with this system is that it is difficult to add extra references, since each only has one number. An additional reference early in the writing means the majority will need re-numbering both in the list and in the text. This can lead to errors. A second drawback with this system is that, if the work is being typed, it can sometimes be difficult to position the numbers slightly above the writing. Many chemistry and physics periodicals and books use this method.

The alphabetical-numerical system

With this system the references are listed alphabetically according to author's surname at the end of any writing and then they are numbered (e.g. 1, 2, 3 etc.). The numbers are then entered in the text at the appropriate places. This system is popular with some academic journals, but great care has to be taken in co-ordinating the references with their correct number. Adding or deleting a reference needs careful checking.

Constructing a Bibliography

Well researched scientific writing always lists, at the end, the sources of information which have been used in its preparation. This list is sometimes referred to as References, Literature cited or Bibliography. The term bibliography is often too loosely used, since a well-prepared bibliography should contain information as to the contents of each reference, in addition to publication details.

The preparation of a reference list always seems to present students with unnecessary difficulty. If, when searching out information, a record of each reference is made on index cards (see p. 9), compiling the list is relatively simple. When required the cards are arranged (removing those not needed) either alphabetically or numerically, and the list is ready for copying out.

Below are examples of different types of information showing what details should be recorded, and how each could be set out in a list. In the examples the Harvard system has been used. With the other methods the same information is required, with the addition of the correct number placed at the beginning of each reference. It is an accepted convention that certain words are underlined (if typed or hand-written) or italicized (if printed). Some authors and publishers recommend slightly different ways of setting out from that given below. For example, the use of capital letters for author's names, reversing the order of publisher and place of publication, and minor changes in punctuation.

The important point is to adopt a system which provides enough detail so that any reader could locate the same reference without any difficulty. Again Examination Boards usually advise on the format required. If the following suggestions are used, it will be relatively easy to alter to the demands of particular Boards.

Examples

Textbook
Record: author(s) surname(s) and initial(s), date of publication, title of book, edition (except the first), publisher, and place of publication. Include page numbers, tables and figures if mention has been made to specific parts of the book.

Fry, A.J. (1989) *Synthetic Organic Electrochemistry* (2nd edition). John Wiley & Sons Ltd, Chichester.

A paper in a periodical
Record: author(s) surname(s) and initial(s), date of publication, title of article, name of journal, volume (and part number if applicable), inclusive pages of paper.

Litinsky, E. (1989) Polynomial integrals of evolution equations. *Communications in Mathematical Physics.* **121** 4, 669–82.

Some journals have long titles and some form of abbreviation is acceptable. However, never make up your own, since if every scientist did this it would soon cause chaos and confusion. Many academic journals use the abbreviations provided in the *World List of Scientific Periodicals* (4th edition, 1963–5, Butterworths) or the *British Union-Catalogue of Periodicals* (BUCOP). The BUCOP began in 1964 and continues the *World List* by including new periodicals published. It appears quarterly with an annual two-volume cumulation. The periodical given above would be abbreviated to *Commun. Math. Phys.* If you are unable to consult a copy of the *World List* or BUCOP then always give the complete titles. In fact, many highly respected scientific journals never use abbreviations and insist authors give titles in full.

With such a large number of periodicals on the market there is considerable variation in the way scientific paper references are set out and some publishers, for example, omit the title of the paper and only cite the author(s) name, date and title of journal. This can make some ILL requests difficult to trace.

A book with every chapter written by a different author
Many books have each chapter written by a different author(s), and the whole book is edited by someone else. In these instances record, for the chapters used: author(s) surname(s), and initial(s), date of publication, title of chapter, inclusive page numbers, together with the surname(s) and initial(s) of the editor(s), title of book, publisher and place of publication.

Winkler, M.A. (1983) Application of the principles of fermentation engineering to biotechnology, in *Principles of Biotechnology*, (ed. A. Wiseman), Surrey University Press (Blackie), Glasgow, pp. 94–143.

A thesis
Record: author surname and initial(s), date, title of thesis, degree awarded, academic institution awarding the degree.

Evans, C. E. (1967) *Some zinc (II) and chromium (III) ionic processes*. PhD Thesis, University College of Wales, Aberystwyth.

A report
The various types of reports have already been described on page 25. Reports can be extremely difficult to trace, since many writers give too little information in their reference lists. Always provide enough detail. If the report has been the responsibility of a particular person (normally the chairperson of the committee writing the report) then classify according to their surname.

Warnock, M. (1984) *Report of the Committee of Inquiry into Human Fertilization and Embryology*. HMSO (Cmnd 9314), London.

If the report has been prepared for an official organization, and the authorship is uncertain, then use the name of the organization in quoting and listing the reference.

Advisory Board for the Research Councils (1983) *Scientific Opportunities and the Research Budget*. A report to the Secretary for Education and Science, Department of Education and Science, London.

Unsigned articles in books and journals
Often articles appear and the author's name cannot be traced. Refer to such articles, both in the text and the reference list, as anonymous together with their date. The word 'anonymous' may be abbreviated to 'anon'.

Anon (1989) New material trips up superconducting theory. *New Scientist*, **122** (1658), 20.

Other books (e.g. data books, directories)
With certain types of reference book it is difficult to find the name of either the editor or author. In such cases give as much detail as possible.

Unpublished information
Although the majority of references will be from published material, occasionally you may learn of some interesting work, possibly in a letter from or during a conversation with another scientist. It is acceptable to use this information, provided the scientist in question has no objection, and you keep this type of reference source to a minimum. Written work relying completely on information from unpublished work would lack credibility. Refer to this type of information source as a personal communication. In the text it would be acknowledged as 'The results of the experiment were not significant (White, pers. comm., 1987)'.

In the reference list the reference should be filed by author in the normal manner, and may include a short description as to the type of communication (for example, 'a letter' or 'conversation'). Many professional publishers instruct their authors to cite this type of source only in the text, and not include them in the reference list. For student work, however, it is good practice to include them in the list; it shows to a reader or examiner that you have consulted a wide variety of different sources.

Non-book sources
In Chapter 3 other sorts of information, apart from books, are described. If you have used some of these they also need listing. Some examination boards prefer non-book sources to be listed separately as 'Non-book' or 'other sources of Information'. With this type of information source, give as many details as possible. For example, with audio-visual material record the title, distribution or production company, date of production or release, production personnel, namely director and producer, and type of material (e.g. film, video, tape, slides). In practice all this information may not be available, so record as much as you can.

Using quotations

It is perfectly acceptable to use quotations to illustrate a particular point in your writing. Always keep each quotation to a minimum, and in general no longer than two or three lines. Quotations of a paragraph or even longer are best left out unless there is a particular reason to include them. Always quote correctly, and acknowledge the source of reference. It improves the presentation if each quotation is indented slightly and separated from the rest of the writing. Use quotation marks, either single ('...') or double ("...") at the beginning and end of each quotation.

Students often fail to realize they can amend quotations to make them more relevant to the writing at hand. For instance, use square brackets if you wish to add something not present in the original quotation, but which would make its meaning clearer. For instance 'They [the crystals] gave off white smoke when heated'. If the author has made a mistake then use *sic* (Latin, meaning 'so written') to show there was an error in the original and you have not misquoted, viz: 'The acid (*sic*) were poured into the flasks'. Here *sic* means that 'acids' should be read instead of 'acid'. Note *sic* is always underlined or italicized. Also if you want to shorten a quotation, but wish to include some of it, then use ... (three dots). For example 'the cat ... on the mat'.

Footnotes

In scientific writing footnotes are normally used to explain an unusual phrase, an unfamiliar term, or add extra information which would be awkward to include in the text. Footnotes are either asterisked or numbered. The numbering is either consecutive throughout the text, or at the start of each page or chapter. Try to keep the use of footnotes to a minimum. Footnote numbers can cause confusion with references if they are also numbered, and, if the work is being typed or word-processed, the spacing of the footnotes at the bottom of the page can be difficult. Social science and humanity students make great use of footnotes, and sometimes use them to quote their references.

Use of *et al.*

Scientific articles and books are sometimes written by more than one author. If there are more than three authors (e.g. Green, Brown, Black and White) then *et al.* (*et alia*, Latin meaning 'and others') can be used instead of quoting all four names. The reference would be referred to by the first author's name followed by *et al.*, for instance, Green *et al.* The reference is quoted in this form in the text, but additional names may be shown in the reference list. The *et al.* is always underlined or printed in italics, and is always followed by a full stop.

Use of *op. cit.* and *ibid.*

Op. cit. (*opere citato*, Latin meaning 'in the work cited') is used when you are referring to a reference which has been mentioned earlier in the text, for instance 'White, *op. cit.*, p. 132'. Normally *op. cit.* is rarely used in science, since references in the text are identified either by reference number, or author and date of publication.

Ibid. (*ibidem*, Latin meaning 'in the same place') is used in the reference list if consecutive references have the same source even though the page numbers may be different.

Boney, A. D. and White, E. B. (1967a) Observations on an endozoic red alga. *J. Mar. Biol. Ass. UK*, **47**, 223–32.
Boney, A. D. and White, E. B. (1967b) Observations on *Kylinia rosulata* from south-west England. *Ibid*, 591–6.

When used, both *op. cit* and *ibid*. are always underlined or italicised.

SUMMARY

This chapter offers advice when writing up your work.
  The key points are:

- writing is an important form of communication and you must be able to communicate clearly and effectively to both scientists and non-scientists about your work
- plan thoroughly before you begin to write
- use techniques like brainstorming and linear plans to help plan and organize your writing
- divide the work into a number of stages to make it easier
- keep to an accepted format for projects and similar assignments
- relate any written work to availability of information
- pay attention to points of style like quoting references, making a bibliography and using quotations, etc.

7

Displaying data: tables and figures

Scientific investigations produce results and it is usually impossible to suitably describe these in words alone. Imagine that 10 volunteers (5 male and 5 female) had their pulse rate measured before and immediately after a 5 minute period of exercise. The results, described in words, might read:

'Volunteer number 1 (male) had an initial rate of 70 beats per minute, and after exercise this had risen to 140 beats per minute. Volunteer number 2 (female) had an initial rate of 78, and after exercise this had increased to 160. Volunteer number 3 (male) had an initial rate of 69, and after exercise, this had risen to 146. Volunteer number 4 (female) had an initial rate of 79 beats per minute ...'.

If this was completed it would make very tedious reading and although the results would be accurately written down they would be very difficult to appreciate. You would need to re-read the passage several times in order to understand what it all meant. The results would be far easier to interpret if set out in a more regular format like a table, or arranged in a figure such as a graph or diagram.

Scientists make great use of tables and figures to display information, and this chapter deals with:

- general guidelines for tables and figures
- using and constructing tables
- using and constructing figures.

7.1 GENERAL GUIDELINES FOR TABLES AND FIGURES

Tables display data in columns and rows, and figures present it in pictorial form. The term figure includes graphs, various charts and all other types of illustration. All methods of display have a number of points in common regarding their use and construction.

○ They are an effective way of describing and comparing data. Correctly used they save on space and do away with boring writing, like the example found at the beginning of this chapter.

○ They help break up the text into readable chunks and make it more attractive to the reader. However, never include smart-looking tables and figures simply because they are expected; they must relate to, and be an integral part of, the work. They should never be used in an attempt to cover up shortcomings and mistakes.

○ In the written text, tables are referred to as 'Tables', and graphs and diagrams etc. as 'Figures'. Both are numbered using Arabic numbers (e.g. 1, 2, 3) and the numbering should correspond to that given in the text. If the work is divided into numbered sections or chapters as in projects, then it is a good idea to incorporate this in the numbering. For example, Table 4.6 would be the sixth table in the fourth chapter or section. With long pieces of writing this type of numbering is less confusing and helps the reader to locate the tables and figures more easily.

○ Always give every table and figure a comprehensive and self-explanatory title. You can make these stand out by underlining, or with different printing styles if done on a word processor.

○ Make them neat and tidy, and a good size, so they are easy to read. Layout is important and any labelling should be accurate and complete. Keep shading to a minimum or it tends to resemble scribble! A good way of shading is to neatly cross-hatch, using a ruler.

○ As far as possible, keep tables and figures near to the relevant part of the text, although this is not always easy to do. Small ones may be included with the writing, whilst larger ones are best on separate sheets, filed close to the relevant section.

○ Numbers are nearly always present and without appropriate units mean very little. Large numbers (e.g., 19 000 000) are cumbersome and best shortened (e.g. 1.9×10^7). If a measure of statistical significance or level of probability is known, it should be stated, either in the title, or as a footnote. If unusual symbols are used, their meanings must also be included in a footnote.

○ In most cases the data used to construct a table or figure will be your own, from either a class practical or project. In other instances you may be re-working data from another source. This is acceptable provided you quote the source, as you would any other reference (see p. 113). If a number of different sources have been used to construct a single table then it is permissible to quote the sources as various (e.g. Table 7.1).

○ There is always the tendency to include too much information in a table or figure. This makes it difficult for the reader to understand, so try to imagine what the reader's first impression would be when you construct any table or figure. Keep them simple and direct.

Constructing tables and figures – the tools you need

You don't have to be a brilliant artist to produce well laid out work. With care, patience and practice, tables and figures are easy to draw. If you can use a compass, a protractor and draw straight lines with a pencil and ruler you have all the skills you need.

You will also require the following pieces of equipment.

○ A set of good quality pencils. Grade HB and B are the best; H and above are too hard and often dig into the paper, making corrections difficult.
○ A pencil sharpener or small knife. Blunt pencils, especially on graphs, tend to produce messy and inaccurate work.
○ A good quality eraser or correcting fluid.
○ A small transparent plastic ruler and set square. These are essential – small ones are easier to manipulate when drawing complex diagrams. A longer ruler and a 'flexicurve' are useful for drawing graphs. Plastic stencils (e.g. scientific apparatus) are available and can be helpful. Plastic drawing instruments become greasy with use and this can mark your work. An occasional wash with mild detergent is a good idea.
○ A pair of compasses and a protractor (circular if possible).
○ A 1p, 2p, and 10p coin. These are easier to trace around than using a compass when drawing small circles for apparatus like round bottom flasks, retorts and evaporating basins. If you need to draw lots of small circles a radius aid is a good buy.
○ If you have to provide the paper, then buy good quality; it stands up to more handling and repeated correcting than a cheaper grade.

Finally, if you have access to a computer with a printer, programmes are available which draw tables and graphs for you. You simply type in the data and the computer does the rest.

7.2 USING AND CONSTRUCTING TABLES

Tables are useful in a number of ways.

○ To display data where numbers are involved. Since tables are constructed in columns and rows it allows numbers to be easily compared, which helps to reveal trends and patterns, and often highlights any unusual results.
○ As actual numbers are quoted, tables are more precise and the reader can pick out individual values. This is difficult to do from figures like pie charts and histograms.

Table 7.1 Examples of non-numerical tables

Example 1: A table showing some of the properties and uses of the halogen elements

Element	Symbol	Atomic number	Colour in gaseous state	Use
Fluorine	F	9	Pale yellow	Rocket fuel
Chlorine	Cl	17	Green yellow	Bleach
Bromine	Br	35	Dark red	Petrol additive
Iodine	I	53	Violet	Photography

Source: Various.

Example 2: A table of Nobel Prize Winners in physics and chemistry, 1930–1940

Date*	Winner	Scientific achievement
1930	C. Raman	Discovery of Raman effect
1932	W. Heisenberg	Quantum mechanics
1933	P.A.M. Dirac	Discovery of new forms of atomic energy
	E. Schrodinger	
1935	J. Chadwick	Discovery of the neutron
1936	V. Hess	Discovery of cosmic radiation
	C. Anderson	Discovery of the positron
1937	C. Davisson	Discovery of the interference phenomenon in
	G.P. Thomson	crystals when irradiated by electrons
1938	E. Fermi	Artificial radioactive elements produced by neutron irradiation
1939	E. Laurence	Invention of the cyclotron

* No prizes were awarded in 1931, 1934 and 1940.
Source: Various.

○ Reference data (e.g. physical constants, government statistics) are mostly arranged in tables. Although it is unlikely you will have to construct a reference table, a working knowledge of tables helps you to use them more effectively.
○ Tables are also used to display other information apart from numbers such as a comparison, or a list of chronological events (Table 7.1).

Good and bad tables

A well laid out table is clear and easy to follow, and assists the reader. Badly constructed, it is difficult to understand and only confuses. For example,

Table 7.2 Table of results

Volunteer	Reading 1	Reading 2
1	70	140
2	78	160
3	69	146
4	79	158
5	70	150
6	80	162
7	71	90
8	75	190
9	72	160
10	79	151

consider again the results mentioned at the start of the chapter. Imagine you are looking at these results for the first time (Figure 7.2) and had not read the earlier paragraph. As they stand you would only have a vague idea of what the results represented. The table lists 10 volunteers and for each one there are 2 readings. No detail is given about the volunteers and the numbers could refer to chocolate bars, bags of cement, or in fact, anything. If a table is to mean something it must be properly laid out.

A better arrangement of the data is in Table 7.3. This contains more detail. The title explains what the results represent and the volunteers have been split into 2 categories. The numbers have been given units and footnotes have been included. If you had to interpret these results, more information could be deduced from the second table than from the first.

Table construction check-list

○ Include a title.
○ Arrange the data in columns (down the page) and rows (across the page). If there are several columns of figures, the first column should be used for the independent variable and the remaining columns for the dependent variables. These two terms are also used when drawing graphs and are explained on page 128.
○ Keep the columns reasonably close together enabling easier comparisons to be made. Each column must have a heading or caption, which should be short and concise. If additional information is needed to explain each caption (or any other part of the table) then use footnotes as in Table 7.3. The footnotes, identified by superscript numbers, are placed at the bottom of the table, normally on the left-hand side.

Table 7.3 The pulse rate of 10 volunteers (5 male and 5 female) taken before and after a five-minute period of exercise[1]

	Pulse rate[3] (beats/min)	
Volunteers[2]	Initial reading	After exercise
Male		
1	70	140
2	69	146
3	70	150
4	71	90
5	72	160
Female		
1	78	160
2	79	158
3	80	162
4	75	190
5	79	151

[1] The exercise consisted of jumping up and down on the spot.
[2] The volunteers were all 25 years old and belonged to the same keep fit class.
[3] The pulse rate was taken at rest with each volunteer sitting in a chair.

○ Divide the columns with natural breaks, although this is difficult with some types of data. Keep the same spacing between rows as with the written parts of the work.
○ Avoid dividing up tables with too many horizontal and vertical lines. This tends to stop the eye from travelling around the page. If you keep the numbers in straight rows and columns this is usually enough to distinguish them.
○ If possible keep a table upright on a page; tables arranged sideways are not so easy to read. Don't let a table spread onto more than one page – is this also difficult to follow.
○ If there is so much data that the final version appears complicated with lots of numbers in many rows and columns then condense and adapt the data. Decide if it is better to draw either several smaller tables or summarize the figures in some way (e.g. percentages, averages, totals). If summary tables are used, the original data should always be retained as it may be required as an appendix (see p. 109).
○ If several tables are being drawn then keep to the same format for each one. This makes the final work more consistent.

○ Quote the source of data if it is not your own.
○ State the units being used. If every value in the table is measured in the same unit, this can be included in the title. If every column contains different units include them in the captions. If possible use SI units (see p. 181).
○ The same advice applies to non-number tables (see Table 7.1). Keep the information in neat rows and columns, provide a title and indicate any reference sources.

7.3 USING AND CONSTRUCTING FIGURES

Figures are useful in a number of ways.

○ Although (apart from graphs) they are not as precise as tables, figures are more eye-catching and have more visual impact. They convey results more directly to the reader.
○ Figures like graphs can be analysed mathematically, and may help in establishing exact relationships between sets of variables.
○ When describing scientific apparatus, a diagram makes the written account clearer to understand. This is true for experimental observations; a drawing (or photograph) is far more convincing than a long, wordy description.

Types of figures

A wide range is available and included here are:

* Graphs.
* Bar charts.
* Histograms.
* Column graphs.
* Pie charts.
* Isotypes.
* Flow charts.
* General diagrams, drawings and photographs.

Note: the rules about layout and construction (e.g. title, neatness, units, size, etc.) apply equally to figures as they do to tables.

Graphs (also termed line graphs, curve charts or line charts)

A graph is an excellent way of showing the relationship between two sets of numbers (known as variables). For example, suppose the volume of water

Table 7.4 The volume of water dripping from a tap during a 10-minute period

Time (minute)	Volume (cm³)
1	4
2	7
3	10
4	12
5	15
6	19
7	21
8	24
9	27
10	30

from a dripping tap was measured after 1 minute, 2 minutes, 3 minutes and so on up to 10 minutes. The results could be set out as in Table 7.4. A far better way of displaying this data would be to draw a graph of volume against time as in Figure 7.1. The line drawn on the graph represents the relationship between the two variables, i.e. volume and time, and shows

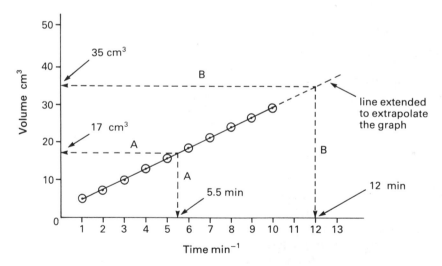

A = Interpolated estimation
B = Extrapolated estimation

Figure 7.1 An example of a graph showing the volume of water dripping from a tap against time (data taken from Table 7.4).

how a change in one relates to a change in the other. In many instances, a curve rather than a straight line is obtained when a graph is drawn.

A graph can be used in a number of ways. Suppose you needed to know the amount of water escaping in 5.5 seconds, a good estimate could be obtained by using the graph without having to repeat the experiment. The estimated value would be 17 cm^3. Obtaining a value within the range of a graph is called interpolation. Alternatively, by extending the line on the graph it is possible to estimate how much water drips in 12 seconds. The value would equal 35 cm^3. Using a graph to estimate a value beyond the range of the original data is called extrapolation.

Parts of a graph

Before advice about drawing graphs is given the names of the various parts need some explanation (refer to Figure 7.2). From the figure you will see that every graph has two axes at right angles to each other; the y or vertical axis

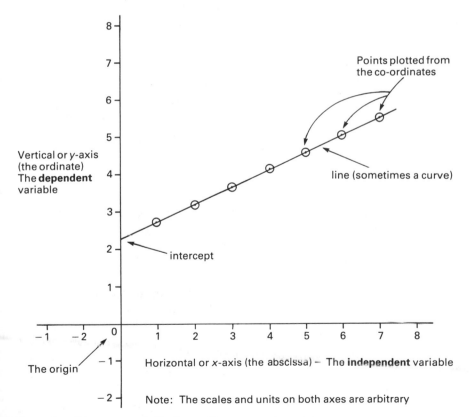

Figure 7.2 Diagram to show the various parts of a graph.

(also termed the ordinate), and the x or horizontal axis (also termed the abscissa). The axes meet at the origin (zero). By extending the axes below and to the left of the origin it is possible to plot negative numbers, and this is needed with some types of data. The x-axis is always used to plot the independent variable, and the y-axis for the dependent variable. Students often confuse the two. The values of the independent variable remain fixed and unchanged by changes in the dependent variable. In an experiment it is the experimenter who gives a fixed set of values to the independent variable. The dependent variable is then measured against these values.

For example, if you (the experimenter) measured the extension of a spring after applying different loads (e.g. 5 g, 10 g, 15 g and so on); the load being under your control would be independent, and the extension, not under your control, would be dependent. Similarly, if you had a hot liquid and measured its cooling at 5-minute intervals up to 60 minutes, the change in temperature would be dependent whilst the time intervals, chosen by you and fixed, would be independent.

A clue in recognizing the two variables is to examine the results being graphed. The independent variable changes at regular intervals, whilst the dependent variable is more irregular. Although with many graphs time is the independent variable and plotted on the x-axis, there are situations where it becomes dependent. For example, when timing a chemical change over a fixed range of temperatures (e.g. 0 °C, 5 °C, 10 °C, 15 °C and so on) time would be dependent and temperature independent.

The pairs of numbers plotted on a graph are called the co-ordinates, and then a curve or straight line is drawn through them. If this is projected to the left, the point at which it touches the y-axis is termed the intercept. With some graphs the intercept reaches the y-axis at 0 or the origin.

Graph construction check-list

o Use standard metric squared graph paper. This is marked off in 1 cm squares which are further divided into 1 mm squares. Some graphs need semi-log paper, and this is described later.

o Decide carefully which is the independent (the x-axis) and dependent (the y-axis) variable.

o Label both axes with the correct quantity and unit involved, e.g. time/s.

o Choose sensible scales for each axis to make the plotting of the co-ordinates as simple as possible. Metric paper is easily divided into 10, or multiples of 10, so that 10 divisions can equal 0.1, 1.0, 10, cr 100, depending on the values being plotted. Avoid a clumsy scale like 10 divisions equalling 3 or 7 or some other odd number; this makes a value like 5.7 difficult to plot.

o Choose a range of suitable scales on each axis, so that the points being plotted are spread out evenly over the graph paper. Excessive manipulation of the scales can make the final graph look strange and give the wrong impression. Both axes should always start at 0 since this prevents misinterpretation. However, if on the vertical axis (*y*-axis) the numbers to be plotted start a good distance from 0 this would cause an empty space at the bottom of the graph. This can be prevented by breaking the vertical axis with a zig-zag line as shown in Figure 7.3. If you use this device never ignore the space at the bottom of the graph, there may be a good scientific reason for it which needs explanation.

○ Plot each point as accurately as possible using either small dots (•) or small crosses (✗). To emphasize each dot set it in a small circle (e.g. ☉). Join up the points with short straight lines using a ruler. If you think the points should all lie on the same straight line, then you need to draw the line of 'best fit'. Either stretch a thread, or place a transparent ruler over the points until it lies evenly between them, and then pencil in the line. This 'eye' method works well if there are a small number of points of fairly high precision. If a large number of imprecise points are plotted, then a mathematical technique known as linear regression analysis may be used. One of the simplest procedures is the 'method of least squares' and all the statistics books listed in the bibliography explain it. Many computer programmes are now available to perform the calculations and some even draw the graph. If a curve needs drawing then if possible use a flexicurve. If you have to draw it free-hand do so from inside the curve, and make the wrist move, whilst keeping the pencil and fingers quite still. A good check to see how well you have drawn a curve is to look along it, at eye level, holding the paper horizontally. Any bumps will be easily seen.

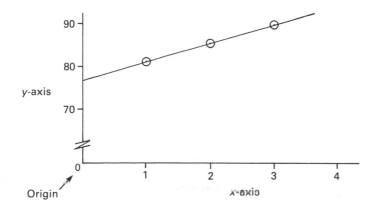

Note: The scales and units on both axes are arbitrary

Figure 7.3 Diagram to show how to break the *y*-axis on a graph.

o During an experiment which requires a graph it is a good idea to plot it as you go along. If the graph appears to be changing shape, e.g. from a straight line to a curve, or if one result seems very different from the rest, it may be possible, depending on the experiment, to repeat that part of the method to obtain a second value as a check on the first. Try to record readings which are spread out evenly over the ranges being investigated unless an intercept value is required, in which case it is best to have several readings close to the axis concerned.

o Like all tables and figures, graphs need to have a title and be numbered. If the data used is not your own then the source of reference must be quoted.

Plotting several curves on one graph

In some situations more than one curve (or line) may be plotted on the same graph. For instance, when calcium carbonate is mixed with hydrochloric acid it produces carbon dioxide gas. The volume of gas (dependent) could be measured at regular time intervals (independent) over a range of different temperatures. A graph of gas volume against time could be drawn and the curve for each temperature plotted on the same axes, rather than draw separate graphs. This would enable easier and more accurate comparisons to be made between the different temperatures.

If more than one curve is plotted, then keep each distinct by using different colours, or having one curve continuous and the others either dotted or dashed, etc. Never put too many curves on the same graph, this will only become confusing.

The uses of straight-line graphs

In science straight-line graphs are particularly useful (e.g. calibration graphs). For instance, if the line passes through the origin, then one variable is directly proportional to the other, i.e. if one is made 2 or 3 times as large, then the other becomes 2 or 3 times as large. Also, if a graph needs to be extrapolated it is far easier to continue a straight line (you use a ruler) than a curve. Not all experimental results, however, produce straight-line graphs. In such cases it is sometimes possible to transform or alter the numbers to produce a straight line without losing any of the scientific sense. Depending on the data, different methods are available.

One way is to construct a semi-log graph. This is where the vertical scale (y-axis) is set out on a logarithmic scale, and the horizontal scale (x-axis) is plotted normally. Hence the term semi-log. Semi-log graphs are useful in that they permit a wide range of values (from very low to very high) to be plotted on the same vertical axis. This is because on a logarithmic scale a doubling on the scale is equivalent to squaring the value involved. Semi-log graphs are also useful if you suspect that the dependent variable shows a constant rate of change. When the graph is drawn a straight line indicates a constant rate. Plotting a semi-log graph is somewhat complicated and you can use either specially printed semi-log paper, or ordinary graph paper. With the latter, it is first necessary to find the logs of the numbers needed for the vertical scale. This can be done with either tables or a calculator. Remember that 0 has no log, so don't put zero on the vertical scale.

There are other ways of producing straight line graphs and these depend on the mathematical equations which describe the relationship between the two variables. These include log graphs, where both axes are set out on a logarithmic scale, and square law graphs where values on the x-axis are squared before being plotted. (Again special graph paper can be used.) In laws of inverse proportion straight lines are produced if the reciprocal numbers for one of the variables is used.

Bar charts

Bar charts, like graphs, have data set against 2 axes and are best used when one set of variables is non-numerical (see example below). Each bar has the same width and it is the height or length of the bar which changes according to the measurement being illustrated. For instance, suppose in connection with the project/dissertation topic described on page 112, a survey had been conducted to investigate energy preferences, and the results were as set out in Table 7.5. Figure 7.4 (Example 1) shows the data arranged in a vertical bar chart. Note that on one axis (energy preference) the information is non-numerical. Bar charts are easy to appreciate and in the example given the different energy preferences are very apparent.

Bar charts may be constructed in a variety of ways (e.g. vertical, horizontal, component, multiple, and back-to-back or change chart) and

Table 7.5 The energy preference of respondents in the survey

Energy preference	Number of respondents		
	Female	Male	Total
Gas	30	50	80
Electricity	10	40	50
Oil	15	10	25
Other forms of energy	15	15	30
Total number of respondents = 185			

Example 1: A vertical bar chart – the bars are drawn vertically and a space is left between each bar.

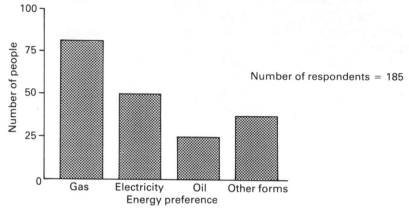

Example 2: A horizontal bar chart – the bars are drawn **horizontally: useful if a large** number of bars is needed, since it is easy to extend the vertical axis.

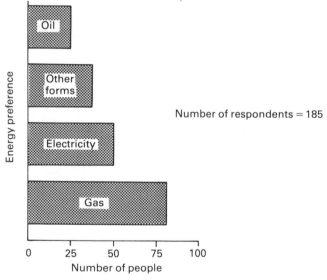

Figure 7.4 Examples of bar chart layouts using the data in Table 7.5.

Figures 7.4 and 7.5 illustrate a number of these, all using the same data. Since so much information can be put into a bar chart there is a tendency to overcrowd them and they lose impact – keep them simple and clear. They can be made to look very attractive with the careful use of colour and shading.

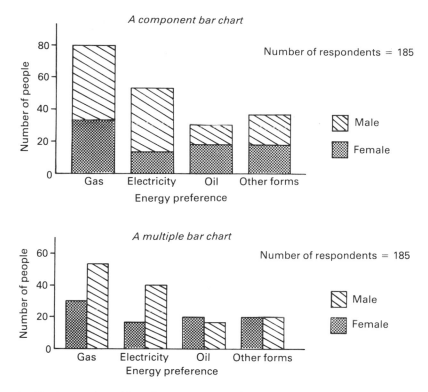

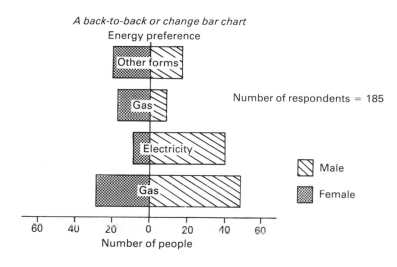

Figure 7.5 Examples of different bar chart layouts using the data in Table 7.5. With these examples each energy preference has been split into male and female.

Table 7.6 Distance travelled in one week by the science students of Pinefield College

Distance (km)	Number of students (frequency)
0 and under 5	10
5 and under 10	18
10 and under 15	20
15 and under 20	36
20 and under 25	16
25 and under 30	10
Total number of students = 110	

Histograms

Histograms are not bar charts, but specialized diagrams to show frequency distributions.

Imagine 110 science students from Pinefield College were asked how far they travelled during one week. The data, when collated, is set out in Table 7.6 and this shows what is termed a grouped frequency distribution. The distances travelled have been arranged in groups (or class intervals) in

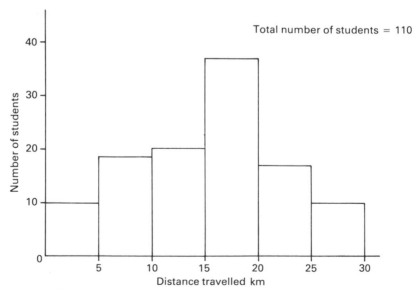

Figure 7.6 An example of a histogram showing the frequency of students and the distance travelled to Pinefield College (constructed using the data in Table 7.6).

order, from the shortest distance to the longest, and the number of students in each class has been recorded. Note the class interval results are continuous (i.e. there are no gaps) and that each class interval has clearly stated boundaries which do not overlap. A student travelling 10 km to college is placed in class interval '10 and under 15', whilst a student travelling 9.99 km would be put into '5 and under 10'. The data in Table 7.6 when drawn as a histogram would appear like Figure 7.6. Histograms are different from other charts in that there are no spaces between each rectangle and the area of each is proportional to the frequency of each class. This means if one class has a frequency twice that of another, then the area of that rectangle will also be twice as much. If you study Figure 7.6 the area of the rectangle above class interval '10 and under 15' is double that above class interval '0 and under 5'.

Column graphs

A frequency distribution which plots discrete data (see p. 166), as opposed to continuous data is termed a column graph. Suppose a plant pathology study has investigated the frequency of plants with different numbers of infected leaves. The results might be as in Table 7.7, which when constructed into a column graph would look like Figure 7.7. These data are discrete because the leaves are either infected or uninfected. In the previous example the data are continuous because any distance could have been travelled by a student on the way to college. With column graphs, because the data are discrete, the

Table 7.7 The frequency of plants possessing different quantities of infected leaves

Number of infected leaves	Number of plants
1	1
2	0
3	3
4	4
5	6
6	8
7	6
8	5
9	4
10	2
Total number of plants = 39	

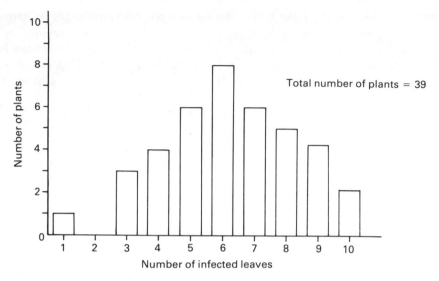

Figure 7.7 An example of a column graph showing the frequency of plants with infected leaves (constructed using the data in Table 7.7).

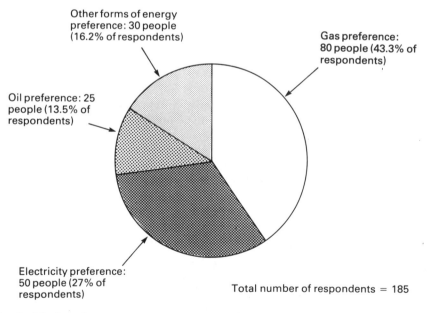

(**Note:** In this chart three sectors have been shaded using different techniques. The largest sector has been left unshaded).

Figure 7.8 An example of a pie chart showing the energy preferences of 185 respondents (constructed using the data in Table 7.5).

rectangles do not touch. As with a histogram, the axes need to be labelled and the whole figure properly headed.

Pie chart (also termed a pie graph or wheel graph)

These are easily understood by the reader and simple to construct. The word 'pie' is used since a circle is divided into sectors, rather like a pie or cake being cut into slices. The complete circle represents the whole sample or 100%, and it is divided up according to the relative size of each component part. They are useful, therefore, if parts need to be compared with the total whole. Pie charts can sometimes be used as an alternative to bar charts. The results in Table 7.5 which have been used to construct the bar charts in Figures 7.4 and 7.5 have also been used to make the pie charts in Figures 7.8 and 7.9.

Constructing a pie chart

○ Draw a circle with the compass set at an appropriate radius. A good size for A4 paper is 5 cm.
○ For each result calculate the angle at the centre as a proportion of the total. In the case of Table 7.5 the total number of answers was 185, corresponding to 360°. Using the results given in Table 7.5 the calculations are as follows:

Gas preference   80 people.

The angle will be $\dfrac{80}{185} \times 360 = 156°$.

Electricity preference   50 people.

The angle will be $\dfrac{50}{185} \times 360 = 97°$.

Oil preference   25 people.

The angle will be $\dfrac{25}{185} \times 360 = 49°$.

Other forms of energy   30 people.

The angle will be $\dfrac{30}{185} \times 360 = 58°$.

(Note: the number of degrees is either rounded up or down to the nearest whole number, i.e. 155.67° becomes 156°.)

Example 1: In this layout one sector (oil) has been slightly removed. This is useful if you wish to give one part particular emphasis.

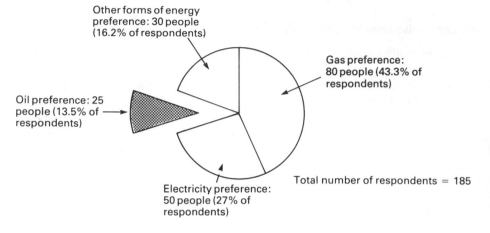

Other forms of energy preference: 30 people (16.2% of respondents)

Gas preference: 80 people (43.3% of respondents)

Oil preference: 25 people (13.5% of respondents)

Electricity preference: 50 people (27% of respondents)

Total number of respondents = 185

Example 2: In this layout one sector (oil) has been divided with the aid of a percentage bar chart to show the male and female response. As with example 1 this is a useful technique to draw attention to one part of the chart.

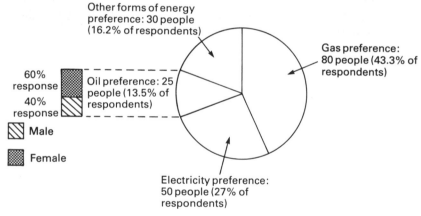

Other forms of energy preference: 30 people (16.2% of respondents)

Gas preference: 80 people (43.3% of respondents)

60% response
40% response

Oil preference: 25 people (13.5% of respondents)

Male

Female

Electricity preference: 50 people (27% of respondents)

Total number of respondents = 185

Figure 7.9 Further examples of pie charts using the data in Table 7.5.

o Using a protractor and starting at the 12 o'clock position, mark off the number of degrees for each preference and draw a line from the centre of the circle to the circumference.

o Each sector is then fully labelled, as in Figure 7.8, and the completed diagram given a title.

Additional points about pie charts

o Each sector may be neatly shaded or coloured for effect.
o Don't divide the chart into too many sectors or it will lose its impact. Four
   or five is usually sufficient. If more parts than this are needed then use a
   bar chart.
o Always include the actual numbers and/or percentages on the chart, since
   this gives it greater precision and accuracy.
o If one sector is particularly small it can look more effective if slightly
   removed from the circle (see Example 1 in Figure 7.9).
o It is sometimes possible to combine a pie chart with a percentage bar chart
   if one sector is particularly interesting and can be divided into further
   categories (see Example 2 in Figure 7.9).
o If a comparison is being made between 2 or more samples, pie charts can
   be drawn with different radii so that the area of each circle will be
   proportional to the size of each sample it represents. For example,
   imagine that a factory producing resistors makes two batches A and B.
   With batch A (1500 resistors) 40% had a high tolerance and 60% had a low
   tolerance. With batch B (1200 resistors) 35% had a high tolerance and 65%
   had a low tolerance. In order to draw pie charts to illustrate this it is first
   necessary to calculate a suitable radius for each sample. This can be done
   as follows:

* Take the larger sample (Batch A) and give it a radius of 5 cm

* The area of the circle for Batch A will be $\pi r^2 = 25\pi$

* To represent 1 resistor would require a circle with an area of

$$\frac{25\pi}{1500}$$

* $\therefore$ to represent a sample of 1200 (Batch B) would require an area of

$$\frac{25\pi \times 1200}{1500} = 20\pi$$

* $\therefore$ the radius of the circle for Batch B is given by

$$\pi r^2 = 20\pi$$

$$\therefore r^2 = 20$$

$$\therefore r = \sqrt{20}$$

$$= 4.47 \quad \text{(to 2 decimal places)}$$

* For each batch you can draw a circle. One with a radius of 5 cm and the
   other with a radius of 4.47 cm. The area of each is proportional to

the size of the sample it represents. You then draw each pie chart calculating the angles in the same way as described for the energy example above. When constructing comparison pie charts always start with the largest sample and give it a radius suited to your needs. This will ensure that the remaining samples have smaller radii and fit on to the paper.

Isotypes (also termed pictographs, pictograms or ideographs)

The word isotype stands for International System of Typographical Picture Education and this method of displaying information was originally developed by Otto Neurath between 1920 and 1945. In an isotype diagram symbols resembling the subjects being counted are used to represent the different quantitites involved. For example, suppose a 4 year study has been carried out to investigate the population changes of domestic cats on a housing estate, and Figure 7.10 represents the completed isotype. Isotypes are interesting to look at and make a useful change from bar and pie charts. The main problem, however, is in drawing the symbols, since they need to be simple, silhouette-like and easy to copy, especially if a large number is needed. They should also look like the subjects they represent. Each symbol stands for a fixed number, and in Figure 7.10 one symbol (🐱) equals 100 cats, and therefore half a symbol (🐱) equals 50 cats. Not all results can be displayed as easily as this. It is difficult to read exact values from an isotype, so always include them on each line as in Figure 7.10.

Flow charts (also termed flow diagrams)

These are useful for illustrating relationships and links between different parts of a subject. They can be used in a number of ways. For instance, to explain the stages in a chemical extraction process, nutrient cycle, life history, or metabolic pathway. When drawing out flow charts never be tempted to make them over-complicated. Keep them large, well labelled and clearly laid out. Computer programmers draw special flow charts when designing programmes, and accepted symbols are used to represent different processes. Be careful not to confuse computer flow charts with other types you may use.

General diagrams, drawings and photographs

Drawings are an important way scientists can record results and observations. You may be expected to draw diagrams of apparatus, and biology students often have to make sketches of different organisms.

The main points to note (in addition to the guidelines on page 119) are as follows.

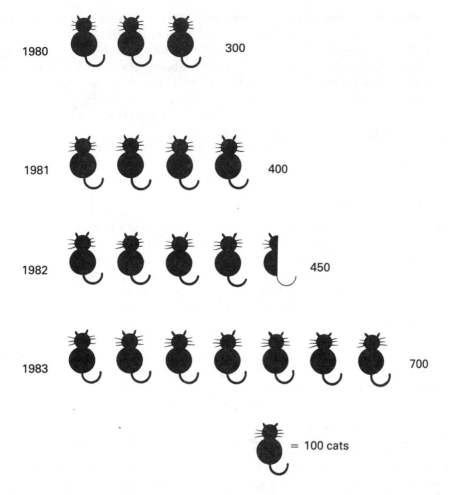

Figure 7.10 An example of an isotype diagram: number of domestic cats on a housing estate, 1980–1983.

○ Keep them as large and clear as possible. Place them in the centre of the page; this will allow plenty of space for any labels and also frame the work.
○ Every illustration needs a complete title, and this should include the view (e.g. side view, surface view). With biological drawings the view is very important and it may be ventral, dorsal or lateral (right or left side).
○ Always provide some idea of scale (e.g. natural size, × 10). Sometimes this is difficult, in which case the words 'not drawn to scale' should appear in the title.

○ Label fully all drawings and diagrams. Use straight label lines from the feature being labelled to the label. End each line at the feature end with either a dot (→•) or an arrow head (→). Make these small and neat, otherwise they tend to obscure the feature being labelled. Keep lines well spaced around a drawing, and never let label lines cross. Some teachers prefer the labels to be on one side (usually the right). As long as the work is well presented, and the labels accurate, use the style you prefer unless directed otherwise.

○ Keep each part in proportion starting in the centre and working outwards seems to help.

Drawing scientific equipment

When describing certain experiments it helps to include a diagram of the apparatus used. With this type of drawing always ensure that if the apparatus was set up from your diagram it would be workable and safe. For example, make sure that corks fit flasks correctly and that delivery tubes are properly connected. To understand this in more detail study Figure 7.11. The top diagram has been correctly set out, whilst the bottom one has been drawn badly.

When drawing apparatus there is often no need to include equipment like a Bunsen burner; the word 'heat' with arrows pointing in the right direction is usually accepted. Although chemistry stencils help, the different parts are sometimes out of proportion and cannot, therefore, be used. Liquids are usually represented by short horizontal wavy lines.

Biological drawings

Biology students tend to make more drawings than other science students and often have to draw specimens while observing them down a microscope. This can be difficult at first, but with practice becomes easier. Try to keep both eyes open taking short glances from the microscope to the drawing and back again. When studying tissue preparations (e.g. a section through a plant stem) two types of drawing are normally required; a low-powered plan and a high-powered drawing. The low-powered plan (so called because the low-power objective is used) should only be a general diagram showing the distribution of the various tissues. Individual cells are only shown in the high-powered drawing (the × 40, or × 100 objective is normally used). Don't include too many cells in the high-powered drawing. Search out the smallest cell you have to draw, make this a reasonable size, and then draw the remainder in proportion. For microscope drawings, unless an eyepiece graticule and slide micrometer are used, it is impossible

Figure 7.11 Drawing scientific equipment – good and bad diagrams.

Good diagram

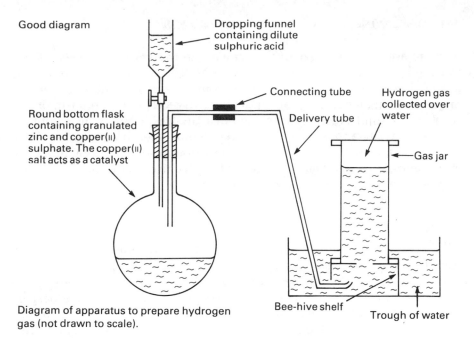

Dropping funnel containing dilute sulphuric acid

Connecting tube

Hydrogen gas collected over water

Round bottom flask containing granulated zinc and copper(II) sulphate. The copper(II) salt acts as a catalyst

Delivery tube

Gas jar

Diagram of apparatus to prepare hydrogen gas (not drawn to scale).

Bee-hive shelf

Trough of water

Bad diagram: the mistakes are numbered and explained below.

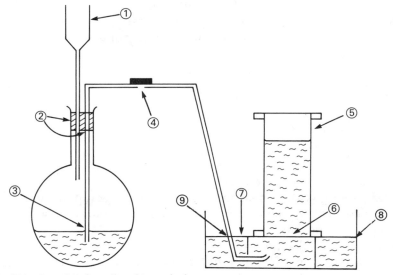

① No liquid in dropping funnel and tap missing.
② Poor fitting cork and blocked delivery tube.
③ The tube is below the level of the liquid. How would the gas escape?
④ Delivery tubes not properly connected.
⑤ Gas jar unstable on bee-hive shelf.
⑥ No hole in bee-hive shelf for gas to pass through.
⑦ The level of water is too low in the trough – the water would run out from the gas jar.
⑧ Water meniscus incorrectly drawn.
⑨ Delivery tube blocked.
Also, there is no heading and scale present. All these mistakes are easily made – they have all been taken from students work.

to relate accurately the size of the drawing to the size of the object being observed, so an indication of the order of magnification is given (e.g. low power, high power, etc.). Remember to include in the title whether the material is a section (radial, tangential or transverse) smear, squash, or the whole organism. Many practical guides are published which contain photographs of various microscope preparations and the drawings which can be made from them. Although these guides are an excellent aid in interpreting microscope slides, never be tempted to copy the drawings. This defeats their purpose.

Photographs

With advances in Polaroid® photography many students are now allowed to use photographs instead of drawings. The basic rules of presentation still apply and all photographs need a heading, labels, and scale. Photographs need mounting into your files or notebooks, using a good quality adhesive. Photographs can be labelled with permanent felt tipped pens and a fine writing grade is the best to use. In the text photographs are usually referred to as 'Plates' and numbered like tables and figures. In a project or dissertation if some special type of photography has been used (e.g. infra-red) a record of the photographic equipment, developing and printing procedures must be noted and included in an appendix.

SUMMARY

This chapter describes how tables and figures may be used to display scientific data.
   The key points are:

- make tables and figures a good size
- keep them accurate, neat and always include appropriate units
- don't overcrowd them or they will lose impact and confuse
- include a title, labels and footnotes etc
- with graphs take care with the axes
- practise drawing the different type of figure (e.g. bar charts, pie charts, etc.), and list the advantages and limitations of each type.

Although this chapter has described a number of ways to display data, you may have original ideas of your own. If so, then give them a try and see what they look like.

8

Giving a talk

Scientists, in addition to writing about their work, often give lectures and talks at conferences and meetings. Such presentations are an important part of scientific communication and many students are now required, during their course, to present short illustrated talks. For example, if you have recently completed a project or dissertation you may be expected to talk about it to the rest of the class. The length for the talk may vary, but it is usually between 15 and 30 minutes, with time allowed at the end for questions from the audience. The talks may be marked and the marks count towards the final assessment in a subject. Like other aspects of studying science, certain skills are involved and this chapter offers the advice needed. The subjects covered include:

- the role of the audience
- format of a talk
- preparation (including the use of visual aids)
- final preparation and delivery
- assessment.

(Reference should also be made to page 76 which describes the type of information needed for a talk).

8.1 THE ROLE OF THE AUDIENCE

The audience is an essential part of any talk. Your content, style and delivery is aimed at them, and you should interest and inform, but never bore. Remember the information you present is to be seen and heard, not read. Bear this in mind during the preparation. Try to imagine yourself in the audience's place and think what it would be like to sit and listen to your talk. This will often help decide the type of material to include. Before the talk try to discover what the audience already knows about the subject. If their knowledge is limited it may be worth including some background material.

On the other hand, if they have a fair understanding then you can start at a higher level. In most cases the audience is likely to be made up of fellow students, so you should know them quite well!

8.2 FORMAT OF A TALK

A talk is best divided into 5 sections:

* Introduction.
* Main part.
* Conclusion.
* Summary.
* Question time.

Introduction

Here you introduce the talk and outline the various subjects which are going to be considered. If using handouts or visual aids, include one at the beginning to list the main areas being discussed. It will give the talk a more structured approach. Use the introduction to establish a relationship with the audience. Even though many may be your friends, standing up and speaking in front of them is a different situation. Adopt a formal, yet friendly manner. You should also use the introduction to go over any background information which may be needed to understand the talk.

Main part

This is where you describe the main information about the topic. Always keep to the same order as given in the introduction and tell the audience when you have finished one section and are going on to the next. When using visual aids explain them thoroughly to the audience. A long pointer will help. Students often prepare excellent visual aids, but never use them to full advantage. They only quickly refer to them and then carry on talking about the next subject. This is off-putting for the audience; they are not sure whether to look at the visual aid or listen to the speaker. It is also wasteful of your time and effort. Remember if you are nervous about talking to a group of people, when using a visual aid the audience looks at the aid and not at you.

  If the talk is either about a project or dissertation, this part is where you explain your methods and results. The visual aids may include graphs, charts and tables. You can also have a demonstration set up of any special equipment that was used.

Time in talks is limited, so pick examples with care. It is better to explain a few carefully, than skim superficially through several. This will only leave the audience confused and possibly bored.

Conclusion

Here you describe the conclusions arrived at in the talk. Again visual aids can be used to list the salient points.

Summary

It is a good idea to finish your presentation with a short summary, highlighting the major issues described. With a book or article readers can refer back to remind themselves of what has gone before. An audience can't do this – they rely on the speaker to tell them. A visual aid at this stage, summarizing the main points, is a good idea.

Question time

Most talks have a question time where the audience can ask about the topics mentioned in the presentation. When answering questions always be honest and if you are not sure of the answer then say so. Never try to fool your audience. If you are well prepared, this is unlikely to happen and question time can be an interesting and enjoyable session.

8.3 PREPARATION (INCLUDING THE USE OF VISUAL AIDS)

As with all your work, sound preparation is the way to achieve a good and professional result. Like other assignments, it is easier to divide the preparation into stages, working at each in turn. The stages are:

* Stage 1: planning the assignment.
* Stage 2: collecting the information.
* Stage 3: sorting out and writing the 'lecture notes'.
* Stage 4: arranging the visual aids.

Stages 1 and 2

These are basically the same as when beginning any assignment. (It may be helpful to re-read Chapter 5, page 77, and Chapter 6, page 92.)

In planning (Stage 1) you produce a brainstorm plan to generate ideas and decide on the information needs. With Stage 2 (collecting the information) you use library retrieval skills to search out and locate information.

If the talk is about a project or dissertation then stages (1) and (2) are nearly complete – you go through the work selecting the parts you need.

Stage 3: sorting out and writing the 'lecture notes'

This is where you sort out the information and structure it into notes which will form the basis of the presentation. Most student talks last no longer than 30 minutes, which means being selective in your choice of material. Possibly you may have collected more than you need. It will not be wasted, but give you a thorough background of the subject. This should make you feel more confident when giving the talk.

Writing 'lecture notes'

When you have chosen which material to include in the introduction, main part, conclusion and summary, you can begin writing your 'lecture notes' to use during the talk.
The following advice should prove useful.

○ Number, underline and annotate as you would all other notes. This helps to consolidate and organize the work.
○ Write notes, not a script. Never read out or learn by heart what you want to say. It will sound stilted, boring and most likely you will speak too quickly. Remember, the audience might need to make their own notes. If you are particularly nervous, it might help just to memorize the opening sentence(s) (**no more**) simply to get started.
○ Make your writing large and clear so that you can read the notes from a good distance. Using capital letters on every other line is one way. Never be 'note bound' and scared to take your eyes off your writing. It will mar the delivery. Some people recommend notes written on cards, rather than paper. Try both and see which you prefer.
○ Keep every sheet of paper (or card) numbered – so if they get moved during your lecture (or you drop them!) you can quickly find your place. It is a good idea to make a hole in one corner and keep the notes together using a treasury tag.
○ Mark the notes where you intend to use visual aids (put VA in the margin).
○ When the notes are complete, practise the talk and time it. Never hold notes (especially if your hand shakes) but put them on a desk, or table in front of you. Speak at a steady pace, sorting out the pronunciation of any difficult and unusual words. A tape recorder is useful here. If you overrun and you think the pace is about right, then see what can be deleted

without losing any sense or order. Often reducing the number of examples, or general background helps sort it out. Timing a lecture accurately is a difficult business – never feel dispirited if it takes a few attempts.

○ If your notes begin to look untidy, don't worry, as long as you can follow them. However, if you think the crossings out and alterations confuse you, and you would be more confident with neater looking notes, re-copy them. It is important to be relaxed and at ease when giving a talk.

Stage 4: arranging the visual aids

It is always a good idea to include visual aids with a talk. They will give variety to your presentation and help keep the interest of the audience. There are different types available and they can be used in many ways:

* To supplement verbal information (e.g. maps, photographs and diagrams).
* To explain experimental results (e.g. tables, graphs and histograms).
* To summarize information (e.g. flow charts, lists and hand-outs).
* To explain complicated situations (e.g. diagrams of metabolic pathways and chemical formulae).
* To build up ideas (e.g. use of overhead transparency overlays).
* To show a technique (e.g. videos and classroom demonstrations).
* To show the application of science (e.g. videos and photographs of industrial processes).

General advice about visual aids

If you are making your own, draw them neatly, following the advice in Chapter 7, page 119. Alternatively, you may be able to borrow certain aids (e.g. videos and 35 mm slides). Many manufacturers produce them for teaching purposes and your college library may have a number. Also the catalogues listed on page 43 could be helpful. Tell the audience whether the visual aids are your own or borrowed and be sure the library (or supplier) knows why you need them. Always verify you are not breaking the law of copyright.

Check that any special equipment like a projector and screen is ordered and that it works. If possible, have spares handy (e.g. a projector bulb) or know how to get a replacement or repair in a hurry in case of a breakdown in the middle of the talk. With all equipment, especially electrical, be sure you know how to operate it (practise beforehand) and check cables and plugs for safety. If you need the room darkened then be sure it has blackout facilities. If not, arrange for an alternative venue.

Types of visual aids

A number of aids are available and those listed below are particularly suitable for student use.

Handouts
Handouts are an excellent aid to a talk and each member of the audience can have their own copies to take away at the end. You can use handouts for many purposes; to provide a summary, for a table or diagram and to list references. Always ensure the handouts are well laid out and neatly arranged. Handouts can be handwritten or typed, and there are many ways they can be copied; photocopying machine, spirit duplicator and waxed stencil duplicator. See what is available and take into account the cost. It is best to distribute handouts at the start of a talk making sure you have sufficient copies. See that everyone is supplied or you may be sure some bright individual will interrupt halfway through to complain they don't have one.

Flip charts
A flip chart is a large pad of paper attached to a board on an easel and when each page is finished it is 'flipped over'. You need special felt-tip pens and bright strong colours (black, blue, red or green) work the best; pale yellows and browns are not very effective. Flip pads are good if you are trying to build up a diagram and involve the audience to give you ideas. They seem to work best in small groups such as seminars. They can be used in any room, needing no electricity or blackout facilities. They are clean to use, unlike chalk boards which can be very dusty. The height of the board on the easel is also easily changed and you can refer back to the earlier sheets if needed. However, unless you have neat handwriting, flip diagrams can look untidy.

Chalk and dry marker boards
Nearly every class, lecture room and laboratory has either a black chalk or white dry marker board, so availability is not a problem. Although good teachers give the impression that using a board is easy, it is more difficult than it looks. Writing on a board and trying to talk at the same time is a tricky business and needs practice. Try to stand diagonally to the board so that you never have your back to the audience. Boards are useful for building up diagrams, spelling out specialist words and terms, and for extra quick sketches if needed at question time. They are good for big groups, provided you keep your handwriting large and clear. If you only have a board available and need a complicated diagram, draw it if possible before the talk. If you want to build up a diagram as your talk proceeds draw it on the board before you talk, and then rub it off. The outline will still be visible very close to the board, but not from a distance. The main disadvantage with any type

of board is that once cleaned, you cannot refer back to a diagram, and with white dry marker boards special pens and cleaning agents are needed. Also chalk boards can be messy and dusty. When using a chalk board always use strong colours like white, yellow and orange. Some makes of red, green and blue chalk can be difficult to see from a distance.

Overhead projector

This is one of the easiest and best aids to use. You draw the figures and tables either on separate transparent acetate sheets, or on an acetate roll, and project them on to a screen or even a pale-coloured wall. No special blackout facilities are needed, although some shading might be necessary in very bright sunlight. You can operate and focus the projector yourself while facing and talking to the audience. You never have to turn away from the audience. Special pens (always keep to strong colours) are needed to write on the acetate. Remember some pens contain permanent ink and mistakes are not easily corrected. Keep the writing large and clear. Make a practice diagram beforehand and look at it from the back of the room to check the legibility. It is also possible to use special acetate sheets which can be used in a photo-copier to reproduce very complicated diagrams from books. Be sure you are allowed to do this.

Overhead projectors are very versatile. For instance, you can use several sheets at once and lay one on top of another to gradually build up a complicated diagram like a chemical pathway, or life history. Some commercial transparencies are available – check what is in your library. The main disadvantage with overhead projectors is that some models can be noisy (because of a cooling fan) and looking at a bright light is sometimes distracting for the speaker, but not for the audience. In addition, if the projector and screen are not correctly aligned, the projected image will appear distorted, with the top wider than the bottom (the 'keystone' effect). This distortion is mostly slight, and does not normally affect the focus and quality of the picture being shown.

Slides, films, videos, filmstrips etc.

A large selection of published slides, videos and film loops is available and can be useful to include in a talk. Depending on the facilities, it may be possible to make your own audio-visual material. Some projectors can be linked to a cassette tape recorder, which can be used to great effect. For example, to show an interview or provide a commentary for an experimental technique. Visual aids using some type of projector, or TV monitor need blackout facilities, and you may need help in turning lights on and off. With a set of slides, enlist the help of a friend to change them during your talk, unless remote controls are available. If there are a lot of slides, a long film, or video decide when is the best time to show them; lights being turned on and off throughout a talk can be distracting. Depending on the topic, it may be best to show them either at the beginning, or towards the end, immediately prior to question time.

Photographs, charts and diagrams
All these are useful provided they are large and can be seen easily. Keep diagrams simple and don't use too many colours. As with an overhead transparency make a practice one and check its legibility from the back of the room. It is best to pin this type of aid up on a board in front of the audience. If any photographs are small they can be passed around, although this can be distracting and they may be accidentally damaged.

Demonstrations
When describing an unusual piece of equipment which you have made, or modified yourself, it is a good idea to show how it works. With demonstrations always practise beforehand and check everything is ready before the actual talk. Demonstrations which go wrong can prove fatal! If you have access to video equipment then play safe and pre-record the demonstration.

8.4 FINAL PREPARATION AND DELIVERY

Finally, there comes the time when you have to stand up and give the talk. The following may help your final preparation and delivery.

o Check that the room is ready, particularly seating arrangements, and that all equipment is in working order.
o Be sure your notes and visual aids are in the correct order.
o Wear comfortable clothes. Although you should be smart and tidy, a talk is not the time to wear a new pair of tight shoes, or shirt with close-fitting collar. If you use reading spectacles be sure to have them with you.
o Expect to be nervous – even experienced lecturers are usually anxious before giving a talk. The important point is to make the nervous energy work for you. Channel it into giving a good talk.
o Address your talk to the entire audience, not just to one teacher or a special friend. Look at all the people present and talk to selected individuals, one at a time, in different parts of the room.
o Speak slowly, clearly and reasonably loud, without shouting. Project your voice to the back of the room and take a deep breath before beginning each sentence. Don't worry about accents. Think of the range of different sounding voices you hear on radio and TV. If you keep steady lively pace, you will sound fine.

o Be enthusiastic and interested in your subject. If you sound bored, the audience soon will be!

o Keep the language simple and direct, explaining any unusual scientific term. Use spoken rather than written English; it is fine to say 'I' and 'you' instead of the impersonal phrases and pronouns used in formal scientific writing. Try to avoid, however, phrases like 'you know', 'that sort of thing' and 'at the end of the day'.

o Refrain from being witty and telling jokes, unless they are good and fit into the material. They may fall flat, and you are not auditioning for a comedy show!

o If possible stand rather than sit. Don't slouch, but keep your weight evenly distributed on both feet. Standing gives you more command over the audience. You will see them more easily, and notice if they begin to look bored and fidgety (quicken and vary the pace) or if they have difficulty in writing notes as you speak (slow down). Use the audience – let them be the guide to govern the speed of your delivery.

o Try to keep reasonably still when talking. Pacing up and down will distract, and habits like jingling keys in your pocket can be off-putting. Don't stand in front of any visual aids when using them.

o Never try to hide your notes; you are not expected to give your talk from memory. As you speak keep taking a quick glance at them to remind you of what comes next. Use them as a prompt.

o All speakers occasionally make mistakes, miss out a point, or accidentally give the wrong information. If this happens what do you do? Never try to carry on, hoping the audience has not noticed. They will soon detect something is wrong, because one mistake tends to lead to another. Be honest and say something like 'I'm sorry I've missed out something, can we go back and pick it up from …'. The audience will appreciate your honesty, and accept the apology. Similarly, if there is a sudden noise or commotion outside stop and re-start when everything seems quiet and calm.

8.5 ASSESSMENT

Any talk you give may be assessed and the mark recorded. Normally two marks are given, the first for content and the second for presentation. The content is judged like any other assignment with marks being awarded for accuracy, the quality of the science and independent thought. The mark for presentation will depend on the style of delivery which includes interest, pace, quality and relevance of visual aids. If the talk is to be assessed then ask your teacher what particular points will be looked for.

SUMMARY

This chapter offers advice about preparing and giving a talk.
   The key points are:
- remember the audience and use them – let them govern your pace of delivery
- thorough preparation is essential – if you have planned and organized the material well, this will help you give a good talk
- have good visual aids and use them to full advantage
- talk from notes not a script
- on the day double-check everything is ready, and stay calm!
- if the talk is assessed, ask how the marks are being allocated.

9

How to plan and carry out projects

Many science courses now expect students to complete an extended and independent piece of practical work. This is usually referred to as a project. Some Examination Boards describe this type of assignment as an 'individual study'. (Long pieces of non-practical work are mostly termed dissertations and these are covered on pages 74–75 and 109–112). This chapter explains some of the things to think about when planning and carrying out a project. These include:

- the value of projects
- choosing a project
- designing the practical work
- the analysis of data
- writing up and presentation.

9.1 THE VALUE OF PROJECTS

When beginning a project, students understandably become concerned about what appears to be a difficult task, which often has to be completed by a set date. Like other aspects of your work, if you make a thorough preparation and complete a stage at a time, a project is relatively straightforward, and the end result is usually of a high quality. Projects are included in courses because they indicate how capable and responsible a student is at working alone, with the minimum of supervision. You should, therefore, regard a project as an opportunity to show your ability in tackling an independent piece of work. A good, well-produced project will demonstrate your competence in a number of ways. It will:

* Be a measure of practical skills, showing how well you handle scientific equipment and follow instructions. It shows whether you adopt safe working practices, essential in all aspects of science.

* Reveal how accurately you observe, measure and record scientific results, and how you present them in the form of tables and figures. It will indicate how you interpret results and compare them with existing work.
* Show your capability in designing a practical investigation with suitable controls and sampling procedures.
* Test your ability to search out scientific information.
* Examine communication skills when you write up (and give a talk about) the project.

In summary, a project provides you with a unique chance to integrate, into one piece of work, skills and knowledge gained from a variety of areas on a course.

9.2 CHOOSING A PROJECT

The stages involved in carrying out a project are similar to preparing any assignment. They are:

* Stage 1: planning the work.
* Stage 2: collecting the information.
* Stage 3: sorting out the information.
* Stage 4: writing up.

Since a project is an extended piece of work, each stage will be longer and more involved than writing up, for example, a class practical. *Stage 1: planning the work*, uses the same skills as when beginning any other assignment. These include the sorting out of ideas and the identification of information needs. Advice on this has already been given in Chapter 5 (see p. 75) and it applies equally well when starting a project. An important part of the planning stage is, however, in choosing an appropriate subject to study.

Types of project

When choosing a topic remember there are different types of practical projects and the word practical does not necessarily imply working in a laboratory.

Experimental projects

With this type of project you do work in a laboratory carrying out either one or a series of experiments to investigate a particular problem. For example, the effect of temperature on the rates of certain chemical reactions.

Observational projects

Many scientific problems involve observing, collecting and analysing data which is already present in some form. An ecologist studying an area of woodland would need to visit the habitat on several occasions, collecting information about the type and number of species present.

Surveys

You may decide to carry out a survey using techniques such as questionnaires and interviews. Although these methods are normally used by social scientists, they are still relevant in science, and can help provide information about people's awareness and understanding of science. If your project intends to consider some of these wider scientific issues then a survey approach is a good one to use.

Which type of project?

There is no reason why a project should not involve a number of approaches. The student studying the woodland (observational), in the example above, may need to bring soil samples back into the laboratory to determine chemical and pH analyses (experimental).
Whichever type of project you select it should:

* Be original and present new information about the topic being studied.
* Contain a critical review of published work, in order to provide a background for the work.
* Show clearly the value and contribution your work makes to the subject as a whole.

Also, when making your final choice, bear the following in mind.

○ Always comply with any course regulations which may specify the type and length of project a candidate is expected to produce.
○ Is there a completely free choice, or must you pick one from a specified list? (with a free choice follow the advice on page 92.)
○ Always relate the choice to the information facilities available. A project is a chance to put to good use the library and information skills described in Chapters 4 and 5.
○ Bear in mind the practical facilities and equipment which are available. It is far better to work on a well devised project using relatively simple equipment than one relying on a complicated piece of scientific technology. Specialist equipment may only be available for a limited time, and could be required by other students.

○ There is normally a time limit set on project work, so choose a topic which can be completed in the time available. You must allow time for the practical work, writing up and presentation. (Chapter 6 (page 102) gives advice on the writing up and arrangement of material in projects.)

○ Discuss potential ideas with one of your teachers. In most cases one member of the teaching staff will act as your project supervisor, providing general and specific advice and may help in selecting an appropriate topic for study. Depending on the course, a supervisor may read through the early drafts of any completed work and provide useful comments and criticisms. A good supervisor should, at the start of a project, clearly set out his or her role and terms of reference. In every case supervisors are only there for guidance, they will not do the work for you. A project is your own work and you must be prepared to demonstrate initiative and commitment to it.

9.3 DESIGNING THE PRACTICAL WORK

At the planning stage it is important to pay attention to the design of the practical work in order to make maximum use of the facilities available. This will ensure that any results are more valid and meaningful. The term 'experimental design' is a general one, and does not only refer to laboratory experiments, but includes surveys and observational projects.

When carrying out a project a number of results will be collected. How do you know if they represent the true situation, or are simply due to chance or some other cause? For example, if an analytical chemist was determining the concentration of sulphur present in a sample taken from a large drum containing a certain compound, the sample might, for some reason, be especially high or low in sulphur. The result might not represent the true concentration of sulphur present in the drum. To guard against obtaining misleading results several samples could be taken and the contents of the drum thoroughly mixed before the start of the analysis. In short, suitable experimental procedures could be selected to ensure that the results were valid and acceptable with a high degree of confidence. This is what is meant by experimental design.

Experimental design is part of a wider subject which can be referred to as 'the scientific method'. This is concerned with the ways in which scientific knowledge develops and advances. Briefly, the scientific method implies that science is studied by a scientist developing a theory, or hypothesis, about a particular topic. In order to see if the hypothesis is correct the scientist designs and carries out an investigation. The results are observed and from them a conclusion is reached whether to accept, or reject, the hypothesis. Many scientists and non-scientists discuss the philosophy and thinking associated with the scientific method and much has been written about it. However, the need for a well designed investigation, in order to study a scientific problem, is equally important for the project student as it is for the Nobel prize winner. Good design provides an opportunity to make accurate comparisons, evaluate data and take into account the magnitude of any errors. The issues you should be aware of when starting a project are:

* The use of controls.
* Sources of error.
* Sampling procedures.
* Choice of suitable techniques.
* Treatment of results.

Many of these issues are inter-related, but are explained separately for ease of description. Depending on your choice of project some will be more important to you than others.

The use of controls

Scientific investigations employ what is termed a 'control'. For example, in an experiment looking at the role of oxygen in the rusting of iron, apparatus could be set up where iron and oxygen were in contact. In order to be certain that any effects observed were due to the presence of oxygen, a similar set of equipment could be set up with iron alone and oxygen absent. This second set would be the control, and must be identical in every respect to the first, apart from the presence of oxygen. A control shows that any observed effect is caused by the treatment being studied and not due to some other factor.

It is essential when designing any practical investigation that consideration is given to the type of controls needed. In many situations it is difficult to devise a simple control. In an investigation on the effect of pH on the activity of a certain enzyme it would be impossible to remove pH since all solutions must be acidic, alkaline, or neutral. In this type of experiment a comparative approach may be taken, and a range of pH, with buffered solutions, used. When using a comparative approach as many conditions as possible, apart from the factor being investigated, must remain constant. In the enzyme experiment only pH will be altered; temperature and solution concentrations etc. will remain the same. The rationale behind a well-controlled investigation is that any results should be able to be reproduced, given the same conditions as in the original study.

Comparative controls are mostly used in observational and survey-type projects, where two or more different situations, or sets of respondents, are examined to see if real differences exist. Sampling methods are obviously important here to ensure that any reported differences are real and not due to variation in sampling technique.

Sources of error

In order to have confidence in results it is important to reduce errors to a minimum, or at least have some idea as to their type and magnitude. They can then be taken into account when you come to write up the work. Some knowledge of the kind of errors which exist helps guard against making avoidable mistakes. The two main types of error are instrumental error and personal error.

Instrumental errors are those inherent in any piece of scientific equipment. All apparatus, whether simple or complex, measures to different degrees of accuracy. The capability of an instrument should be known at the start of an experiment. For example, if you wish to record temperature over a narrow range it is better to use a thermometer calibrated to tenths of a degree rather than single degrees. Instrumental error can be reduced be ensuring a piece of equipment is correctly set up at the start of an investigation.

Personal errors can also occur. A common one is that due to parallax. This is the effect which causes an apparent change in the position of an object due to a change in the position of the eye. Parallax is involved when measuring the length of an object using a ruler, or when estimating a value where a pointer lies mid-way between two marked divisions on a fixed scale. It is also present when measuring the volume of liquids with pipettes, burettes and measuring cylinders. Personal errors, although never completely eliminated, can be reduced by adopting correct techniques and by taking a number of readings.

Sampling procedures

Irrespective of the type of project you will rely, in most cases, on the use of samples to obtain results. For example, when analysing the chemical composition of a substance, only a small portion or sample would be needed. When conducting a survey, you would not question every individual but hopefully a small, representative number. The ecologist studying a habitat would not look at every plant and animal, but again at a small sample.

Samples are used to save time and money, because in most investigations it is impossible to examine every individual and/or situation. Samples are used, therefore, to make predictions about the population or case as a whole. As a consequence any sample must be truly representative; if not, any deduction made, as a result of studying the sample, would be wrong and misleading.

To some extent the number and type of samples required in an investigation depends on the natural variation present. Chemists and physicists are fortunate here, since with much of their work any variation is minimal. Imagine a student who was carrying out a series of experiments with sodium chloride and required daily samples. If all samples were taken from the same jar there would be little difference between them. Biologists, however, are not so lucky. Living organisms, even of the same species, exhibit enormous variation. Look around at your colleagues in class. You all belong to the same species, but some of you will be tall, some short, fat, thin, dark, fair etc. If you were volunteers in a physiological experiment, how would you know if the final results were due to the conditions of the experiment or the natural variation present? In any project, therefore, the sampling procedure must take into account any variation which may influence the outcome of the investigation.

Depending on the nature of the work there are no hard and fast rules about the number of samples to use. Generally, it is best to take as many as possible in the time available, ensuring they are chosen without bias and truly representative of the population. If you intend to use some statistical test of significance then the number of samples must be decided upon at the start of the project. The choice of test is often governed by the number of samples. Like experimental design, different sampling methods can become complex, and the bibliography lists references should you require specialist advice.

Choice of suitable techniques

Projects test practical skills and your ability to choose suitable techniques for the topic being studied. The following covers a number of general and useful points, together with specific advice for experimental, observational and survey projects.

General advice

○ Take a careful and disciplined approach, working out everything in detail before you start. Make a list of all the apparatus needed, including simple equipment (e.g. test tubes, filter paper, beakers). Arrange to order chemicals and specialist equipment, bearing in mind the cost and time available. Your supervisor should help with the general arrangements for laboratory space. Some colleges provide technical help, whereas others expect the students to do everything for themselves.
○ Plan the work schedule well in advance and if you need specialist equipment be sure it is available when needed. Also, make sure you know how to use it.
○ Adhere to any safety regulations and guidelines.
○ Pay attention to the recording of results. If you have to make continuous readings over long periods, how will this affect your other work? Do you need permission to work out of normal hours (e.g. evenings and weekends)?

○ If time allows, have a preliminary run through the techniques (often called a pilot study). This helps you become familiar with any new methods and identifies points of difficulty. Analyse any collected data to determine if the chosen statistical tests and other quantitative techniques are suitable. A run-through enables you to make modifications before the main investigation begins.

Experimental projects

Most experimental projects are laboratory-based, and the following will apply.

○ To avoid errors follow all experimental procedures precisely, paying attention when weighing, making up solutions, and handling equipment and chemicals.
○ Always use good quality equipment and glassware, especially if very accurate measurements are needed.
○ Keep glassware clean and dry.
○ Obtain permission to leave out any equipment between experiments, and always leave your bench space clean and tidy.
○ Dispose of all waste safely and never leave toxic or hazardous chemicals unattended.

Observational projects

Many observational projects take place in a laboratory and safe working practices still apply. Observational projects record information which is already present (e.g. the description of an animal or plant). With this type of investigation always make a detailed check list of every feature you wish to record – this ensures that no point is missed. Ecological projects (also observational) usually include some field work which must also be thoroughly planned. You should:

* Obtain permission to visit the chosen habitat.
* Go properly clothed (e.g. waterproofs and strong footwear), and take a map and other necessary equipment.
* Keep specimen collection to a minimum. Always respect and conserve the environment. Wildlife and Countryside Acts restrict what can be collected.
* If possible go with a companion: be sure to tell your college and colleagues where you are going, and at what time you expect to be back.
* Carry a card with emergency telephone numbers: a whistle can also be useful.

Survey projects: designing questionnaires

A survey asks a number of people (the respondents) their views and opinions about various issues, and in recent years this type of investigation has become popular with scientists. Scientific discoveries such as radioactivity have a profound effect on society. It is important to gauge and monitor their impact. Like other scientific projects, surveys need thorough preparation and must be properly thought out. A friendly chat with a group of people does not constitute a survey! The methods used to collect and evaluate data must be as well planned as any laboratory experiment.

A successful way to collect information is to use a questionnaire. This can be used either in an interview, or the respondent can complete it privately at home. In large surveys, postal questionnaires are sometimes used. They can, however, be difficult to arrange and are best avoided unless there is some special reason for using them. The return of postal questionnaires tends to be low and, therefore, produces few results.

A questionnaire is basically a series of questions; each question providing a number of alternative answers from which the respondent can choose. The wording of the questions is very important, since the choice of answers provides the results on which you base your conclusions. When preparing questionnaires always remember the following points.

○ Keep the questions in a logical order. The wording should be direct and simple.
○ Answers should fall into distinct categories which, if possible, should be indicated by a tick. For example, in a survey investigating energy preference (see p. 112) a question might read:

Please tick (√) the following energy sources used in your home:

Gas	
Electricity	
Oil	
Other forms (e.g. coal)	

○ If a questionnaire is to be answered by a respondent privately, as opposed to asking questions in an interview, then layout and presentation are important. It should be neat and attractive to look at. Don't make it too long – 2 or 3 pages at the most. Arrange to collect the completed questionnaire, or provide a prepaid envelope for posting back.

○ Never ask personal, emotive or leading questions. For example, 'Don't you think electrical energy is the best sort to have?' Rather, ask 'Which type of energy do you prefer?' and provide a list of types with boxes for the respondent to tick as in the example on the previous page.
○ Include a short introduction to tell the respondent what the survey is about and why you are doing it.
○ When designing a questionnaire decide at the beginning how you intend to interpret the results. Survey data are often expressed in percentage terms and can be illustrated in bar and pie charts. Chi-square analysis is a common statistical test used in surveys.
○ Choose the sample of respondents carefully to avoid any bias. This is often difficult to do. Suppose the project involved surveying students enrolled on a particular course at your college. You would need to include an equal number from every class and, if appropriate, an equal number of both sexes. The whole population in a survey is termed the sampling frame, and it is from this frame that a representative sample is chosen.
○ Always stress to every participant that any information given is confidential and that anonymity will be respected. Remember to thank everyone who takes part. It is a good idea to make available the final project for them to read if they so wish. A copy could be left in your college library.
○ If time is available a pilot questionnaire can be helpful. This is an early draft of the questions, tried out on a few selected volunteers (friends and relatives will do). This exercise will pick out difficult and ambiguous questions, and your volunteers' comments will help to make the final questionnaire more direct and precise.

To give a better idea of what a questionnaire looks like study Figure 9.1. It is the first page of a questionnaire used by the author in an investigation on biotechnology in Humberside.

Treatment of results

At the planning stage it is essential to decide the form the results will take and the methods you intend to use to analyse them. This will strengthen the design of the project and support the validity of any conclusions. Too many scientists only think about results and what to do with them when projects are up and running. If any statistical tests are being used, you must know, at the start, how many samples are needed and how they will be measured; most tests can only be used with certain types of data.
With regard to results, consider the following points.

Figure 9.1 An example of a questionnaire used by the author when carrying out a survey.

BIOTECHNOLOGY IN HUMBERSIDE

This questionnaire is part of a larger study designed to assess the use made of Biotechnology within the County of Humberside. As with most questionnaires some of the questions may seem superfluous or irrelevant. We have tried, however, to make the questions as short as possible, and each question has a particular research objective in mind.

Most of the questions can be answered by placing a tick in the appropriate boxes.

Remember that your answers will remain absolutely confidential, and will not be associated with your identity at any stage.

We should welcome any comments on any aspect of the questionnaire and on any other points you may wish to make. Space has been provided at the end for this purpose.

If you do not want to take part in this survey please write your address in the following box. We will remove you from our mailing list and you will not be contacted again.

```
Address_____

        _____

        _____

        _____

Post code  _____
```

Question 1.

Before this questionnaire were you already aware of "Biotechnology"?

Please tick the appropriate box	Yes	
	No	:

If you ticked YES then please go to Question 2 and complete the rest of the questionnaire.

If you ticked NO, but would like to know more about Biotechnology and how it could influence your business then go to Question 12 on the last page of the questionnaire.

Question 2.

Where did you first hear about Biotechnology?

	Radio	
	Television	
Please tick the appropriate box	Newspaper/ Magazine	
	Other source	
	Don't know	:

If you ticked "Other source" please state source:-

_____

Question 3.

Have you taken part in any other survey about Biotechnology?

Please tick the appropriate box	Yes	
	No	

○ Remember, the equipment you use could restrict the type and number of results, which in turn may limit how they can be analysed. Always choose a suitable technique of recording results.
○ Decide whether you are recording either qualitative or quantitative data (see p. 106).
○ Qualitative results may be recorded by drawings, short notes, photographs and videos. Chapter 7 (see p. 140) gives advice about drawings and diagrams.
○ Quantitative data involves numbers and these are best recorded in table format. Although raw data may need to be summarized and undergo various calculations, the principles of table construction still apply (see p. 121). Decide which units to use and what every result stands for, so that when you come to sort them out you will have a better understanding of what everything means.
○ Quantitative data is either discrete (e.g. a football team can only score 1, 2, 3, 4 goals and so on, not 3.5 goals) or continuous, i.e. a variable may take any value (e.g. height or weight).
○ Decide which scale of measurement to use. If statistical tests are needed this is very important. The different scales are:
   * *Nominal or categorical*, where data are sorted according to category and each variable can only belong to one category (e.g., sex, blood grouping and colour).
   * *Ordinal*, where data are sorted according to rank and order; individuals are classified into exclusive groups and then each group is arranged in order (an example would be four political parties, each getting a share of the vote in an election, and then arranged in order of votes cast).
   * *Interval*, a scale where there are equal differences between points on the scale, but there is no true zero – the zero point is arbitrary (e.g. time and temperature.)
   * *Ratio*, similar to an interval scale, but there is a true zero (e.g. length.)

9.4 THE ANALYSIS OF DATA

When carrying out the practical work for a project you will be collecting and recording your results.

○ Do so accurately and be clear in your own mind what has to be measured and observed.
○ Be honest and never be tempted to falsify results.
○ Keep proper records in a file or notebook. Work on scraps of paper is easily lost or mislaid. With longer assignments it is a good idea to make a copy of results by using carbon paper. One copy may be left at college, the other taken home. All teachers have come across students who lose data.

With a short assignment, although troublesome, it is not impossible to do it again. With longer-term investigations, lost data can be fatal.

○ Quickly draw graphs and make calculations etc. as you go along. This will give some idea as to the general trend the results are taking, and may alert you to the need for extra readings. This may be too late if left until later, by which time the apparatus may have been dismantled, or in use with another class or student. Many computer programmes are now available which will draw out various figures and make calculations. Use them if available – they save a great deal of time.

With a project you will also be collecting library information and making notes from different reference sources. It can often seem very rushed and chaotic, with several things happening at the same time. Keep calm – this is where thorough planning really helps. You will see at a glance what is finished and what still needs to be done.

You also need to think about analysing and interpreting your results. Always try to have a clear idea of what you think they should show. For instance, a comparison, or the relationship between one variable and another. Try to relate how your results agree or disagree with the work of other scientists. At this stage study any graphs and figures you may have drawn, and see if they show any trends or patterns. This is also the time to carry out any statistical tests.

Use of statistical analysis

The word statistics covers the use of presenting information in a numerical form, in order to obtain a better understanding of the information. It includes graphs and diagrams, already described on page 119, and these may be termed descriptive statistics. There are also inferential statistics where various mathematical formulae are applied to the sample data, and as a result estimates and predictions are made about the population from which the samples are taken. Many subjects, like social science and geography, as well as science use statistical analysis. The intention here is not to give a detailed account of the various tests available, but rather offer general advice. (The bibliography recommends specialist statistics books.) If you wish to use any statistical test in a project you must decide at the start which test you intend to use. This is because many tests may only be used with certain types of data in terms of scale of measurement and number of samples. Also note that the application of statistics will not improve poor results, but rather highlight any discrepancies and faults.

Applying a statistical test (sometimes called tests of significance)

Tests of significance do not prove a particular set of results to be right or wrong. They give a measure of probability that the results from an investigation have not arisen because of chance alone, but represent the true situation present in the population. All tests are carried out using the same basic scheme.

○ A null hypothesis (referred to as H_0) is first set up. This states that no significant differences exist between the sets of data under investigation. For example, this could be data from a particular experiment and the control, or results from two different survey samples.
○ An alternative hypothesis is also set up (referred to as H_1) which states that a real difference exists between sets of data. For example, the control and experimental results are different, and genuine differences exist between the two survey samples.
○ The chosen statistical test is then carried out (e.g. Student's t-test, z-test, chi-square analysis etc.) and a calculated value is obtained.
○ The calculated value is then compared to the value in the probability tables, specific for the particular test being used. The level of probability (p) is also chosen and in most scientific investigations a probability level of 5% or 0.05 is used. If the calculated value is less than that quoted in the table the null hypothesis is rejected in favour of accepting the alternative hypothesis. This implies that significant differences exist. If the probability level is 0.05 this means that in 95 cases out of 100 the results are due to real differences existing between the sets of data being studied, and in 5 cases out of 100 they are due to chance.

All this at first reading may appear somewhat complicated. However, if you decide at the start which test to apply, then statistics should present no real problem. Calculators make the arithmetic fairly easy and many computer programmes are now available which make the whole procedure simple. One final point, don't confuse the null hypothesis with the hypothesis mentioned in connection with the scientific method (see page 158) – the two are not the same.

Choosing the appropriate statistical test

This is the most difficult part and, if you have never studied any statistics, it is a good idea to discuss the whole thing with your project supervisor. Statistics properly used and applied can be very useful. If wrongly used they mean very little and can be misleading. All the statistics books quoted in the bibliography give advice regarding the correct choice of test. The following may also help you in choosing a suitable test.

○ Decide if you need a parametric or non-parametric test. Parametric tests (sometimes called distribution-free statistics) refer to data which do not belong to a fixed type of distribution. Generally nominal or ordinal data require this type of test. Parametric tests assume the data belong to a fixed type of distribution (e.g. normal distribution etc.).

o Are you comparing two small samples (each less than 30) or two large samples (each more than 30)? The Student's t-test is good for small samples and the z-test for larger ones.

o If you need to compare more than two samples a method involving the analysis of variance (often abbreviated to ANOVA or ANOVAR) may be needed.

o If your findings are comparing an observed result with an expected result, then chi-square analysis may be suitable.

o Correlation co-efficients and regression analysis are useful if you need to investigate the relationship between two variables. Regression analysis is also mentioned on page 129 in connection with straight line graphs.

9.5 WRITING UP AND PRESENTATION

This has already been discussed in Chapter 6 (see p. 102). Some colleges expect certain students (e.g. undergraduates) to have their work professionally bound like a book, in which case always go to a good book-binding firm. It can be an expensive business, so obtain a quotation beforehand. Many libraries offer a binding service using a loose-leaf plastic spiral fastening and this is acceptable for many courses. Presentation is important so be sure it is done well.

SUMMARY

This chapter is about projects and the issues to consider when planning and carrying them out.

The key points are:

- plan the work very carefully before you start
- choose the type of project you want to do – is it experimental or observational, or do you want to carry out a survey?
- work out all practical details before you start the work
- design the investigations with care, noting the use of controls, sampling methods, etc.
- decide what the results will be like and what tests, if any, will help analyse and interpet them
- make a good job of writing up and presentation.

10

Assessment and examinations

At some point in your course, normally towards the end, all your marks will be collated and graded and, if satisfactory, the qualification awarded. With most science courses the final grade is arrived at by considering a student's overall performance in both course work and examination. This is termed continuous assessment and has a number of advantages for the student. First, it is fair as all apsects of your work are taken into account. Secondly, as course work is marked as the course proceeds, you can monitor your progress. If you are getting good marks this should encourage you, although don't become complacent. If the marks are disappointing, this will help you identify and sort out the parts you find difficult.

The ratio of course work to examination depends on your course. The type of assessed course work may also vary; it might be entirely practical work, or a combination of written and practical assignments. There are also different forms of examination ranging from traditional theory to open-style papers. Any assessment will, however, always test a range of objectives such as those listed in Chapter 1 (see p. 1), although every objective will not be tested in each assignment.

You may wonder how your work is marked and what teachers look for when going through a piece of work. You may also query how the students' work at one college is compared with those at another who may be entered for the same qualification. When marking an assignment a teacher devises a mark scheme, which takes into account the particular objectives being assessed, and allocates marks accordingly. For example, the mark scheme for a project may award marks for literature review, planning and organization, experimental design, execution of practical· work, interpretation of results, quality and presentation of the written report and quality and presentation of the talk.

Comparing work from different centres is achieved in a number of ways. Examination Boards like the Business and Technician Education Council (BTEC) appoint experienced teachers to act as moderators, who visit several centres around the country. Universities and other institutes of higher education (e.g. polytechnics) appoint external examiners who vet assessment methods and the standard of marking. All this helps ensure parity between students.

Although course work is used to determine final grades on most courses, examinations (theory and/or practical) are still important and most students become anxious at the thought of them. Sitting in a room, with other students, having to write for up to 3 hours can be a daunting experience. Few would describe it as a pleasure, although with planned revision, examinations do become less stressful. Regard them as a challenge, like some sporting event; like all challenges, they need preparation. A good sprinter would never turn up on the day of the race and expect to run well without first having gone through a training schedule. Examinations are no different; if you want to succeed you need to have worked at a planned programme of revision. This chapter offers advice about examinations and covers:

- planning the revision
- types of examinations
- strategies to adopt before, during, and after an examination
- emergency measures.

10.1 PLANNING THE REVISION

Revision should present no problem if you have worked consistently and conscientiously throughout the course; checking notes and preparing assignments are in themselves revision. It is wise, however, when drawing up the study timetable, at the start of a course, to set aside time for examination work. Begin revision as soon as possible, at least 8 weeks before the first examination. The more time you devote to revision the easier it becomes and the more confident you feel. Use the following scheme when planning revision.

○ Make a list of every topic which may be examined. Include both theory and practical work. Even if there is not a separate practical examination, work carried out in practical classes may still be questioned in theory papers. Write all the topics into your study timetable. Don't spend one week solely on one subject, but give yourself variety when revising. Divide each subject into manageable chunks which can be worked through in study sessions of about 2 hours. Guard against giving favourite topics more time than the rest; devote an equal amount of time to each one.
○ Keep to the same pattern of working: repeated periods of 30 minutes, followed by short 5 minute breaks (see p. 11).
○ Make revision an active not a passive process. The emphasis must be on the recall and re-organization of information, not simply reading notes.

As you work through notes (including those made for assignments) write out lists and summaries which condense the material. These summaries may already be done (see p. 13), but it is a good idea to copy them onto postcards as these can be looked at on the bus or train. The more times you go over a subject the easier it is to recall. Keep testing yourself as you work through each topic, and ask a relative or friend to help you.

○ Learn basic material like formulae, definitions, derivations and laws very well. Practise from memory drawing out labelled diagrams of apparatus, chemical pathways etc. Keep looking back at the notes if you are not sure – this helps the process of recall.

○ Revise all related topics at the same time. Look for connecting themes and ideas which could form the basis of an examination question. This helps the re-organization of material.

○ Well before an examination read through previous examination papers. Go back, if possible, about 5 or 6 years and study the type of questions set. (With new courses Examination Boards usually provide specimen papers.) You may find that certain topics are always examined in a similar way. Use this to help you revise. Practise writing out outline answers. Very rarely do questions ask for a straightforward regurgitation of lecture notes. They require material to be compared, discussed and explained etc. This is why when revising you need to spend time re-organizing the information, as well as trying to recall it. Questions which ask for an account of an experiment usually need some mention of results and how you would interpret them. Examination Boards spend a great deal of time in checking the wording of questions. Attention is paid to making them as unambiguous as possible. Even so examinations tend to use a terminology all of their own and Table 10.1 lists some of the words often found in examination questions.

○ Most Examination Boards publish reports which often highlight common errors made by candidates. If you are allowed to look at these, they may help you guard against making the same mistakes.

○ Depending on your background it may be sometime since you sat an examination. If so, then give yourself a mock examination by completing

Table 10.1 Some common words used in examinations, and their meanings

Account for	Give reasons for a particular situation.
Amplify	Expand and enlarge on a situation.
Calculate	This is used when a numerical answer is required. Always show all the working.
Classify	Put into an order.
Comment	A brief account picking out the important points only.
Compare	To examine points of similarity and difference between two or more situations.

Table 10.1 *Continued*

Contrast	Describe the differences between two or more situations.
Criticise	A reasoned account of the good and bad points present.
Deduce	An alternative to predict.
Define	A precise explanation, usually in one or two sentences.
Describe	Give a straightforward account, usually with diagrams.
Determine	Often used as an alternative to calculate.
Discuss	Implies a critical account noting the advantages and limitations present.
Distinguish	A reasoned account separating two or more things.
Enumerate	Give a list of reasons for a particular situation.
Evaluate	A reasoned account describing the good and bad points.
Explain	A reasoned account of why a particular situation occurs.
Find	Often used as an alternative to calculate.
Function	Appears in questions such as 'What are the functions of . . .'. It means you have to describe the jobs and duties a particular thing does. Not to be confused with mathematical functions.
Give	The word 'give' often appears in examination papers and it means 'provide'. It is what you have to provide which is important; is it a discussion, explanation, description, criticism etc? Always read the question carefully.
Illustrate your answer with reference to	Describe examples to back up your answer. It does not mean, in this context, to draw a picture.
Importance	Often used as an alternative word to function.
List	Give a catalogue of points.
Measure	Find a quantity, again show all working.
Outline	An alternative to summarize.
Predict	From the information given in the question, describe what you think may happen in a given situation.
Prove	From the evidence available show how a particular situation occurs. The proof may be mathematical in some cases.
Review	Provide a well reasoned account describing the whole situation and picking out good and bad points.
Relate	Describe how one thing fits in with another.
Significance	An alternative to either function, or importance.
State	Often used as an alternative to define.
Suggest	Give reasons for something.
Summarize	Provide a brief outline of the situation.
Trace	Provide a logical and ordered outline.
Write	'Write' is a command like 'give' and it is what you have to write that is important. Read the question!

an old paper in the set time allowed. This is excellent revision, giving you a good idea of what it is like to work under examination conditions.

o Practise numerical problems and data exercises which may be set.

o Mnemonics can often be used to remember facts. For example, the well known sentence 'Richard Of York Gave Battle In Vain' helps recall the colours of the spectrum (Red, Orange, Yellow, Green, Blue, Indigo, Violet). Make up your own mnemonics; they are easy to do.

o Another aid to memory is to draw a regular shape over each summary diagram. For example, if a topic is in 5 sections then draw a large 5-pointed star on top of it. You will remember the shape, which in turn will remind you that the topic is in 5 parts. Any shape will do as long as it is regular and angular (e.g. square, diamond, triangle, zig-zag). Irregular doodles don't seem to help much.

o It is a good idea to revise with other students. For example, if 3 or 4 students can get together at a regular time, they can each take a turn at leading a discussion on a particular subject, with the others joining in to ask questions. You can set each other short tests and work through old examination papers. Sessions like this consolidate your learning and, being in a group, provides a change from working alone. These groups must be run well, with each student working hard and contributing equally. They must not degenerate into a general gossip session simply to moan about the course, teachers and examinations in particular!

o Finally, ignore students who broadcast loud and long that they have revised everything at least half a dozen times, and examinations are dead easy. It is more likely their revision is disorganized and going badly. Be an independent learner, confident of your own skills and ability.

10.2 TYPES OF EXAMINATIONS

It is important when revising to know the format of every paper you have to sit, and exactly what is required in terms of type and number of questions to be answered. Examinations vary and in addition to the traditional theory paper, consisting of a limited choice of questions (usually 5 from 8), there are short-answer and multiple-choice papers. Some Examination Boards refer to examinations as phase tests and end-of-unit assessments; open papers are also used. An open examination is one where the students are given the paper sometime before the official date of the examination. They then use the intervening time to prepare their choice of questions, which are then written up, usually without notes, at the set date and time. Although an open paper might appear easier, the questions are always more searching, requiring a greater degree of interpretation and discussion. Finally, some science courses still require students to sit practical examinations and these are described on page 175.

Points to note about your examinations

○ How many papers are there on each subject? If there is more than one, does each paper examine the whole syllabus, or are certain topics set on particular papers? This is useful for last-minute revision.
○ How long is each paper and how many questions must be attempted? Is there a free choice of questions, or are some compulsory?
○ What is the mark distribution on each paper? Does each question carry an equal number of marks and does the distribution equate to the time allowed for each question? For example, if a compulsory question is supposed to take you a third of the time, does it carry a third of the marks?
○ Is every question of the same type or can a paper be a mix of descriptive, multiple-choice or short-answer questions? Many science examination papers now include data interpretation and analysis questions. The student is given experimental results and required to comment and interpret them with the aid of graphs, tables and charts, etc. If you have to answer this type of question, then bear in mind the advice given about tables and figures in Chapter 7, p. 119.

The answers to most of these points are given in the official regulations published for each course. Your teacher should keep you informed.

Practical examinations

Most courses now assess practical skills continually throughout the course, rather than by examination. If, however, you do have to sit a separate practical examination then the advice already given about revision still applies. In addition, the following will also help:

○ With practical papers there is usually no choice and every question needs to be attempted. If there are a large number of candidates, equipment may have to be shared or allocated to you for a fixed amount of time. At the beginning of a practical examination be quite clear what you have to do – careful planning is very important.
○ Practical examinations consist mainly of tests of technical skill, small experiments, identification of materials and specimens, and interpretation of results. Normally you will have carried out similar exercises in class, so take your time and never panic. If you think a piece of apparatus is incorrectly set up, and not working properly, then ask the invigilator for assistance. Many things can go wrong in a practical examination which are not the fault of the candidate; you will be not be penalized for them.
○ Always work safely and carefully. Wear a clean laboratory coat and use safety spectacles. Some practical examinations award marks for the way

you conduct yourself in a laboratory (e.g. keeping the bench tidy and using the correct techniques when handling equipment).

○ Most marks are given for your completed written answers, which are collected in at the end, so leave as much time as possible for the writing up of each question. Again if you have to draw tables and figures then follow the advice in Chapter 7, p. 119.

○ Some practical examinations allow you to take in and use any textbooks, lecture notes and practical files. If so, then before the examination, during your revision, go through everything you intend to take in with you. For practical files and notes write out a detailed contents page. This will enable you to find information quickly; many students spend so long during the examination searching through files and notes that they leave themselves short of time to write their answers!

10.3 STRATEGIES TO ADOPT BEFORE, DURING AND AFTER AN EXAMINATION

Before an examination

After all the hard work the examinations arrive and the time spent on revision can be put to good use. Don't worry about feeling nervous; it means you are geared up and ready to start. Most students sit a number of papers over a one- or two-week period, and once the examinations have begun there is little you can do in terms of new revision. Between papers relax and rest, but if you feel you need to do extra work then go through your summary diagrams and revision notes.

The night before an examination collect together all your pens, pencils and materials needed for the next day. Remember to pack your laboratory coat if there is a practical exam. Never work too late; go to bed reasonably early and get a good night's sleep.

On the day of the examination remain as relaxed and calm as possible. On your way to the examination avoid discussing the forthcoming paper with fellow students. If you feel you must do some last-minute revision then choose one topic and slowly read it through. Never jump from subject to subject, this will only confuse you. Rather get your mind into a steady and concentrating mood.

Arrive at the examination room with time to spare – last-minute rushes tend to cause panic. Examination rooms are usually formally laid out with rows of desks and chairs. If there are a large number of candidates several different subjects may be taken at the same time, with a seating plan directing students where to sit. Find where your place is.

During an examination

Once you are seated and have received the writing and question paper you will be told to start. Keep calm and remember the following points.

○ Check you have been given the correct question paper. Invigilators sometimes make mistakes, especially if several subjects are being examined at the same time.
○ Carefully read the instructions (sometimes called the 'rubric' or 'Directions to Candidates') at the top of the question paper. You may know already, but it is a wise precaution to check.
○ If you have a compulsory part to answer then start with this. There is little point in attempting the rest of the paper until this is finished. If the compulsory section consists of short-answer or multiple-choice questions, complete those you can do immediately, and any which seem difficult leave to the end. Even if after a second attempt there are still questions you cannot answer, then have a few intelligent guesses. Some of these may turn out to be correct and will score marks; unanswered questions score zero!
○ If there is a choice of questions read the paper slowly and carefully, deleting those which you think are especially difficult, or on subjects where your revision has been limited. Pick questions on topics which you have thoroughly revised. Provided you number every answer clearly, questions can usually be attempted in any order.
○ Having made your choice

1. Study the wording and underline the key words (e.g. describe, explain, compare etc.). Let the question help plan your answer. For example, imagine that in a chemistry examination a question reads: 'Explain how zinc is extracted from its chief ore, and describe a test to distinguish zinc oxide from magnesium oxide'. This question is in two parts, and you need first to give an account of the extraction, followed secondly by a description of a test to distinguish between the two oxides. A good answer might begin 'The chief ore of zinc is zinc blend, ZnS, and the metal is extracted as follows …'.

    When this account is finished, the second part of the question could begin, with a new paragraph, 'A test to distinguish between the two oxides is …'.

    This question is **not** asking the candidates to write all they know about zinc, yet many students attempting this type of question would produce long, rambling, essay-type descriptions about zinc. An answer should not be an essay unless the question specifically asks for one. For example, 'Write an essay on the extraction and importance of zinc'.

2. With every question decide exactly what needs to be done, and the main points you wish to include in the answer. It is a good idea to plan and sort out every question before you begin to write any answers. This may seem a brave thing to do, but once it is done, nearly all the thinking and sorting out is complete. Your question plans will also help recall when you come to write up each answer.

3. If a question contains a numerical problem always show the working, unless directed otherwise. Marks are given both for a final value and the way it is calculated. Check any calculations carefully to avoid silly mistakes. If you find some formulae particularly difficult to remember, then write them down at the start of the examination as soon as you are told you are allowed to write. Then if you need them you have them ready and very little time has been wasted if they are not required.

4. Include diagrams etc. in an answer if they are relevant. Many papers, in the rubric, advise candidates to include them. A well labelled diagram is quicker to complete than a long description. Make any diagrams large (at least half a page) and neatly labelled, with a heading. The advice given on page 140 about drawing diagrams applies even in examinations.

○ Although science examinations are not testing English, and few marks will be deducted for the occasional mistake, write as well as you can. In particular spell scientific terms correctly, and keep numbers, formulae and symbols clear. Keep work as neat as possible and make your writing legible. Although examiners are not marking neatness, they cannot award marks for work they cannot read.

○ Time each question as precisely as you can. If there are five questions to be attempted in 3 hours, this gives about 35 minutes per question. It allows 5 minutes for planning, 25 minutes for writing, and 5 minutes for a final read through. The latter is very important. When writing at speed the occasional word may be missed out which can change the whole meaning of a sentence.

○ Always attempt the required number (never more) of questions. If you are supposed to complete five, but have only answered four, you will be automatically marked at zero for the fifth question. Some questions are split into several sections, so again check that you have attempted every part.

○ Remember to number clearly each answer and each part of an answer. The numbering should correspond exactly to that given on the examination paper. If you can see that you are going to need more writing paper then ask for it in plenty of time. With some examinations, candidates are instructed to begin each question on a fresh sheet. Be sure your name (and examination number) are on every sheet, and at the end of the examination the sheets are numbered and arranged in the right order. Some Examination Boards use specially printed stationery and provide treasury tags to keep answers together.

○ After finishing an answer you may cross through any plans and rough work; never cross out any part of an answer because you think it is poor. Examiners only mark what is right, not what is wrong. What you consider poor might be worth a few marks! Also never obscure your plans. Showing you have planned a question creates a favourable impression.

○ Examination rooms can become stuffy and hot. Always wear comfortable clothes.

○ Put your hand up and tell the invigilators if you have any problems, such as a distracting noise outside, or you feel ill. They may be able to help.

After an examination

When you leave the examination forget all about it until you receive the results. Stay away from students who insist they did a wonderful job, with first class answers to every question. Have a good rest, and then get ready for the next examination if you have one. Be business-like and efficient in your attitude. It all helps increase confidence in your ability to do well. With internal examinations you may have your answers returned with comments. Study them carefully, and see where marks were lost and gained. This will help when you revise for the next set of examinations.

10.4 EMERGENCY MEASURES

Suppose you are required to complete five questions, but only think you know enough to answer four. What do you do about the fifth question? First, re-read your completed questions making sure the answers are the best you can do and they contain no slips or obvious errors. Secondly, read carefully the remaining questions on the paper and pick the one you know most about. If the syllabus has been completely covered you should know something. Having made your choice start writing all you know about the subject and keep writing until you are told to stop. Your answer will obviously be poor, unplanned, and contain a lot of 'waffle', but by chance it may score one or two marks. No attempt at a question scores zero. The few marks gained may make all the difference between one grade and the next, and even between pass and fail. Writing 'waffle' goes against all the advice given in this book, but sometimes there is no alternative!

What should you do if you miss an examination because of a sudden illness, accident or breakdown in transport? The first thing is to contact the examination centre immediately informing them of the situation. If transport is the problem, arrive at the centre as soon as possible and extra time may be allowed. If you are ill get a friend or relative to telephone the centre and then arrange to see a doctor as soon as possible, obtaining a certificate detailing the illness. Send the certificate with an explanatory letter (keep copies) to the examination centre. Examination Boards have different procedures to deal with emergencies, but are very fair with genuine problems.

SUMMARY

This chapter explains all about examinations and how to prepare for them. The key points are:

- find out all you can about your examinations (e.g. number, type, format of papers, etc.)
- be organized and revise in plenty of time – make a revision timetable and stick to it
- make revision an active not a passive process
- emphasize recall and re-organization
- working with other students, if organized is a good way of revising
- adopt sensible strategies before, during and after an examination
- take emergency measures if necessary.

Appendix I: SI units

Nowadays scientists are recommended to use an international system of units, referred to as SI units (Système Internationale d'Unités). With certain units, however, there is still considerable variation and most Examination Boards provide guidance for candidates.

There are seven **basic units** and two **supplementary units** (see Table AI.I). Each unit can be defined. For example, the kilogram is the unit of mass and is equal to the mass of the International Prototype (a platinum cylinder) kept at Sèvres near Paris. All other units in the system are called **derived units**. They are formed by the multiplication and/or division of one or more of the basic units. Some of these derived units, when expressed in terms of the basic units, become complex and are, therefore, given special names. For example, electrical resistance, in terms of basic units, would be $kg\ m^2\ s^{-3}\ A^{-2}$. It is easier to refer to this as the Ohm and its symbol is the Ω. Some derived units are not given special names (e.g. the SI unit for area is the square metre and the symbol is m^2). There are a large number of derived units and most physics textbooks list the commonly used ones.

NOTES ABOUT USING UNITS

Multiple units

In order to express multiples or fractions (or sub-multiples) of the basic units a set of standard prefixes is used (see Table AI.2). For example, the metre can be prefixed as follows:

Prefix and metre	Symbol	Length in metres
kilometre	km	1000
centimetre	cm	0.01
millimetre	mm	0.001
micrometre	μm	0.000001

Table AI.1 Basic and supplementary units

Physical quantity	Name of unit	Symbol for unit
Basic units		
Length	metre	m
Mass	kilogram	kg
Time	second	s
Electric current	ampere	A
Thermodynamic temperature	kelvin	K
Amount of substance	mole	mol
Luminous intensity	candela	cd
Supplementary units		
Plane angle	radian	rad
Solid angle	steradian	sr

When using prefixes note:

* There is no space between the prefix and the unit (i.e. cm **not** c m).
* Multiple prefixes are not used; for example, with 10^{-9} m use nm **not** mμm.
* Care must be taken to distinguish between capital and lower case letters. For example, M is the symbol for mega (10^6) and m the symbol for milli (10^{-3}).

Table AI.2 Standard prefixes

Prefix	Symbol	Multiple
exa	E	10^{18}
peta	P	10^{15}
tera	T	10^{12}
giga	G	10^9
mega	M	10^6
kilo	k	10^3
hecto	h	10^2
deca	da	10^1
deci	d	10^{-1}
centi	c	10^{-2}
milli	m	10^{-3}
micro	μ	10^{-6}
nano	n	10^{-9}
pico	p	10^{-12}
femto	f	10^{-15}
atto	a	10^{-18}

* An exponent used with a unit refers to the whole unit, i.e. $1\,km^2$ means $1\,(km)^2$ **not** $1\,k(m)^2$.
* The kilogram (a basic unit) is already prefixed. The symbol, kg, is taken as a complete unit, and multiples or fractions of the kilogram are attached to the symbol g, even though the gram is not a basic unit.

Decimal notation

Decimals are shown by using either a full stop (.) or a comma (,). In the UK a full stop is used and other metric countries use a comma. The decimal point is placed on the line (i.e. 4.7). With a value less than 1, the decimal point should always be preceded by a zero (e.g. 0.34).

Thousand marker

Since the comma may be used as a decimal marker, it is best not used to separate thousands. Instead a space can be included, although with four-digit numbers it is usually omitted (e.g. 1234). Five digit numbers and above are thus written 12345, with spaces left between each group of three numbers. However, if five digit numbers and above are included with smaller numbers (e.g. in tables etc.) then it is a good idea to leave spaces with all numbers (e.g. 1234, 12345). This makes the numbers easier to read and compare.

Unit symbols

In general the symbols for the units are written in lower-case letters unless the symbol is taken from a person's name, in which case a capital letter is used, for example, m (metre) and A (ampère). The exception is the litre which is either L, or l. The capital letter is preferred, since l may be mistaken for the number one (1) in some situations. Also note that a symbol remains unaltered in the plural (i.e. 4 m **not** 4 ms) and it is never followed by a full stop unless it is at the end of a sentence.

The solidus (/)

In tables and figures the solidus is mostly used to separate a quantity from its unit, for example, time/s. Although some journals and books use this style in the written text, some scientists prefer the solidus not to be used, and the above example may appear as 'time (second)', 'time per second', or 'time s^{-1}'.

Energy

The term calorie is never used and energy is measured in either joules (J) or kilojoules (kJ).

Time

The basic unit for time is the second (s), although in some situations it is more convenient to use hour (h), minute (min), day or year. There are no accepted symbols for day and year, and these are best written out in full.

Temperature

The basic unit for temperature is the kelvin (K), and this should always be used in physical chemistry and thermodynamic calculations. Other branches of science use the celsius scale (°C) for everyday use and convenience. This causes few problems since, by definition, one degree on the Celsius scale has the same 'size' as one degree on the Kelvin scale.

Volume

Although many journals and textbooks retain the ml and the L or l, the preferred units are the cm^3 and dm^3.

Concentration

This is best written, for example, as 0.3 mol dm^{-3} **not** 0.3 M.

0-333-383729 ⟶ £6.99

0-333-597885 ⟶ New ed. 9/93

Bibliography

The following, listed by chapter, are recommended if you need additional advice and information. The details for each were correct at the time of writing, although it is always worth checking to see if later editions are available.

2 BASIC STUDY SKILLS

A large number of study skills books are published. Unfortunately, few are specifically written for the scientist, the majority being for the humanities and social science student. The following titles are, however, good and well worth using.

Barrass, R. (1984) *Study! A Guide to Effective Revision. Study and Examination Techniques.* Chapman and Hall, London. This book contains lots of helpful advice.

Casey, F. (1985) *How to Study: Practical Guide.* Macmillan Educational, London. This has a useful chapter on different reading techniques.

Ellis, R. and Hopkins, K. (1985) *How to Succeed in Written Work and Study: A Handbook for Students.* Collins, London. This covers a lot of ground and a very detailed contents makes the book easy to follow.

Habeshaw, S. and Steeds, D. (1987) *53 Interesting Communication Exercises for the Science Student. Interesting Ways to Teach No. 5.* Technical and Educational Services, Bristol. This book contains 53 exercises for you to try; they are worth working through if you have the time.

Race, P. (1983) *Study Science Successfully.* National Extension College, Cambridge. This book, written for scientists, is very good, but you need a lot of time to work through all the examples given.

The National Extension College at Cambridge also publish a series of short and easy to read guides. The following are worth looking at:

Freeman, R. (1972) *How to Study Effectively.*

Sullivan, T. (1979) *Studying.*

Sullivan, T. (1979) *Writing.*

Sullivan, T. (1979) *Reading and Understanding.* — out of print

3 SOURCES OF SCIENTIFIC INFORMATION

Many of the following books, in addition to describing the various information sources, cover library organization and information retrieval.

General books

Grogan, D. J. (ed.) (1982) *Science and Technology; An Introduction to the Literature* (4th edition). Clive Bingley, London. A very good text with a useful section on trade literature.

Hoffman, A. (1986) *Research for Writers*. A. & C. Black, London. Although written for the professional writer, this book is excellent – full of common sense and ideas. There is an extensive reading list and a long list of addresses of libraries and information services, etc.

Parker, C. C. and Turley, R. V. (1986) *Information Sources in Science and Technology* (2nd edition). Butterworths, London. A comprehensive book, useful for the undergraduate and postgraduate student.

Specialist books

The following are recommended for the specific areas of science.

Biology

Wyatt, H.V. (ed.) (1987) *Information Sources in the Life Sciences* (3rd edition). Butterworths, London.

Chemistry

Maizell, R. E. (ed.) (1987) *How to Find Chemical Information – A Guide for Practicing Chemists, Educators and Students* (2nd edition). John Wiley, New York.

Physics

Melton, L. R. A. (1978) *Introductory Guide to Information Sources in Physics*. Institute of Physics, Bristol and London.

Shaw, D. F. (ed.) (1985) *Information Sources in Physics* (2nd edition). Butterworths, London.

4 LOCATING SCIENTIFIC INFORMATION: USING LIBRARIES

Many of the books listed for Chapter 3 contain information about library organization. In addition, the following book provides more specialist advice.
Harrison, C. and Beenham, R. (1985) *Basics of Librarianship* (2nd edition). Clive Bingley, London.

5 IDENTIFYING INFORMATION NEEDS

No specific texts are recommended for this chapter, since the books listed for Chapters 2 and 3 contain helpful advice.

6 SCIENTIFIC WRITING

A large number of books are published offering help about writing reports, scientific papers, points of style etc. The following titles are thought to be particularly suited to the needs of the science student.
Barrass, R. (1978) *Scientists Must Write: A Guide to Better Writing for Scientists and Engineers*. Chapman and Hall, London.
Booth, P.F. (1984) *Report Writing: Guidelines for Information Workers.* Elm Publications, Kings Repton, Cambs. This covers all aspects of report writing and Chapter 6 includes reports for special purposes.
Bryson, B. (ed.) (1987) *The Penguin Dictionary of Troublesome Words* (2nd edition). Penguin, London. This is an excellent little book, and explains clearly when to use words like 'stationery' and 'stationary', etc. There is also a good section on punctuation.
Dodd, J. S. (ed.) (1986) *The ACS Style Guide – A Manual For Authors and Editors*. American Chemical Society, Washington, DC. This again covers everything there is to know about scientific writing. There is a useful Appendix V on 'Hints to the Typist' should you need your work professionally typed.
Ebel, H. F., Bliefert, C. and Russey, W. E. (1987) *The Art of Scientific Writing: From Student Reports to Professional Publications in Chemistry and Related Fields*. VCH Verlagsgesellschaft, West Germany. This book covers everything you need to know about scientific writing.
Evans, D.W. (1986) *Improving English Skills*. Pitman, London. This is an excellent basic English grammar book, clear and easy to understand. It is well worth looking out for.
Farr, A. D. (1985) *Science Writing for Beginners*. Blackwells, Oxford. This is a good book for student use, and Chapter 9 covers word processing.
Turk, C. and Kirkman, J. (1988) *Effective Writing – Improving Scientific, Technical and Business Communication* (2nd edition). E. & F. N. Spon, London.

This is an excellent book with a number of chapters giving advice on general presentation of scientific writing.

7 DISPLAYING DATA: TABLES AND FIGURES

Most of the general study skills and statistic books recommended contain chapters on drawing tables and figures. The following two titles, although not written for scientists, are especially good and well worth using, and are easy to follow.

Chapman, M. (in collaboration with B. Mahon) (1986) *Plain Figures*. HMSO, London. An excellent and detailed text covering tables, graphs, charts etc. This is a really definitive guide about the display of data.

Page, G. T. (1983) *How to Present Information Visually and Colourfully. Institute of Manpower Studies; Report No. 55*. Institute of Manpower Studies; University of Sussex, Brighton. Although produced for business management personnel, this is an excellent little book and one of the best on the market.

8 GIVING A TALK

Many of the books listed for Chapters 2 and 6 contain sections on delivering lectures and talks. In addition the following books are recommended.

Booth, V. (1985) *Communicating in Science; Writing and Speaking*. Cambridge University Press, Cambridge. Chapter 3 of this book concentrates on speaking at conferences and preparing talks.

McPherson, A. and Timms, H. (1988) *The Audiovisual handbook – A Complete Guide to the World of Audiovisual Techniques*. Pelham Books, London. A big glossy book which, although written for the professional film maker, has some good advice even for the student and is worth looking at if available.

Powell, L. S. (1970) *A Guide to the Use of Visual Aids* (3rd edition). British Association for Commercial and Industrial Education, London. A short but excellent book on all aspects of visual aids.

Smithson, S. and Whitehead, J. (1987) *Business Communication*. Financial Training Publications; London. Although written for the business studies student, this book contains an excellent chapter (Chapter 8) on giving a talk.

9 HOW TO PLAN AND CARRY OUT PROJECTS

General books

Bennett, N. (1983) *Research Design; Educational Studies. A Third Level Course. Methods of Educational Enquiry Block Two*. Open University Press, Milton

Keynes. Although written for education students, Part 1 of the book covers hypothesis formulation. It is easy to read, and will be useful for all types of investigation. Part 2 of the book covers sampling procedures and will be helpful if you need to prepare surveys and questionnaires.

Pentz, M. and Shott, M. (ed.) (1988) *Handling Experimental Data*. Open University Press, Milton Keynes. A book with a good general chapter on the planning of experiments. It also contains advice about drawing tables and graphs.

Weast, R. C. (ed.) (1988) *CRC Handbook of Chemistry and Physics. Student Edition*, CRC Press, Inc., Florida. This is an excellent reference book for all science students with details of nomenclature, physical constants, formulae etc.

Wedgwood, M. A. (1987) *Tackling Biology Projects*. Macmillan (Published in Association with the Institute of Biology), London. Although written for the biology student it contains excellent advice for all types of scientific projects.

Health and safety

Bretherick, L. (1986) *Hazards in the Chemical Laboratory* (4th edition). Royal Society of Chemistry, London.

Hawkins, M. D. (1988) *Safety and Laboratory Practice* (3rd edition). Cassell Publications Ltd, London. A really good book covering most aspects of safety. It is easy to read and understand.

Statistics

The following titles cover basic statistical fomulae and procedures, and most of them include chapters on drawing figures and tables.

Chatfield, C. (1983) *Statistics for Technology: A Course in Applied Statistics* (3rd edition). Chapman and Hall, London.

Harper, W. M. (1987) *Statistics* (5th edition). Macdonald and Evans, London. An extremely easy to understand book, with all formulae well explained.

Miller, C. J. and Miller, J. N. (1984) *Statistics for Analytical Chemistry*. Ellis Horwood, Chichester.

Phillips, D. S. (1978) *Basic Statistics for Health Science Students*. W. H. Freeman, San Francisco. An easy to read book. Chapter 2 is good on ratios, proportions, percentages and rates.

Porkess, R. (ed.) (1988) *Dictionary of Statistics*. Collins, London. This dictionary explains clearly the statistical terms and types of tests available.

Wardlaw, A. C. (1985) *Practical Statistics for Experimental Biologists*. John Wiley, Chichester. This book contains useful keys to identify which statistical test to use and will be useful for all students, not just biologists.

10 ASSESSMENT AND EXAMINATIONS

The books listed for Chapter 2 contain sections on revision and examination techniques.

APPENDIX I SI UNITS

Modern advanced physics textbooks contain sections on the use of SI units. The various academic institutes also publish guides. For example:
Biological Nomenclature: Recommendations on Terms, Units and Symbols (1989). The Institute of Biology, London.
This booklet has been produced in consultation with various commercial publishers and most Examination Boards. You can buy a copy by writing to:

The Institute of Biology
20 Queensbury Place
London   SW7 2DZ

For definitive advice about units consult:
Quantities, Units and Symbols in Physical Chemistry (1988) – Produced by the International Union of Pure and Applied Chemistry (IUPAC) and prepared for publication by Mills, I., Cvitas, T., Homann, K., Kallay, N. and Kuchitsu, K., Blackwells, Oxford.

Index

Only pages where useful information is given about a topic are included, passing references are usually omitted. Some of the more useful books mentioned in Chapters 3 and 4 are also listed. Page numbers set in italic type refer to figures and tables.